The Eleventh Commandment

Freedom through Forgiveness

The Eleventh Commandment

Freedom through Forgiveness

Andy Smith

Word Aflame Press
Hazelwood, MO

WORD AFLAME PRESS

THE ELEVENTH COMMANDMENT

by Andy Smith

© 2006 Word Aflame Press
Hazelwood MO 63042-2299
Cover design and layout by Andy Smith and Shane Long
Cover photo by Stephen Peeck
Printing History: 2006

Scripture quotations marked "NIV" are taken from the NEW INTERNA-
TIONAL VERSION®. Copyright © 1973, 1978, 1984 International Bible
Society. Used by permission of Zondervan. All rights reserved. Scripture quotations marked "NKJV" are taken from the New King James Version®. Copyright
© 1982 by Thomas Nelson, Inc. Used by permission. All rights reserved.
Scripture quotations marked "KJV" are taken from the King James Version of
the Bible.

Printed in the United States of America

WORD AFLAME PRESS
8855 Dunn Road, Hazelwood, MO 63042
www.pentecostalpublishing.com

Library of Congress Cataloging-in-Publication Data

Smith, Andy.
    The eleventh commandment : freedom through forgiveness / Andy Smith.
       p. cm.
    ISBN 1-56722-685-X
    1. Forgiveness—Relgious aspects—Christianity. I. Title.
    BV4647.F55S63 2006
    248.8'6—dc

                              2006004944

To Mom and Dad

Your departure proved to be the genesis of this book.
God used your passing to initiate a healing ministry
that otherwise never would have existed.
I love you. I miss you.
I forgive you.

OTHER TITLES BY ANDY SMITH

All the Colors
(Yet to be released)
ISBN: 0-9748149-0-3

Empowered...By Pleading the Blood
Paperback – ISBN: 0-9748149-3-8

The Eleventh Commandment:
Freedom through Forgiveness
Audiobook (CD) – ISBN: 0-7577-32917

The Scent of Anointing:
Equipping Men for Exceptional Living
Paperback – ISBN: 0-9748149-1-1
Audiobook (CD) – ISBN: 0-9748149-2-X

CONTENTS

FOREWORD

Sometimes you just need someone to put his arm around you and comfort you. But sometimes you need someone to look you in the eye and tell you the truth. I thought I was doing just fine with forgiveness until I sat with a small group of ministers and listened to Andy Smith challenge us to deal with areas of our lives that we had covered up. It really hurt. But what kept me from feeling beat up was that he let us know that he was a fellow traveler, still working through these same issues. Andy Smith writes like he talks. In your face. At your heart. To your spirit. Your experience with the book when you read it might not be pretty, but it will be good.

David S. Norris, Ph.D.
Professor of Biblical Theology
Urshan Graduate School of Theology

CHAPTER ONE

HOPE FOR A CHANGE

We drove down the road and discussed our future. I told her that I was going to change.

She looked at me from the passenger's seat and said that I could never stop having sex with her. At that moment, in my mind, I agreed. I couldn't really argue because that was the way it had always been. There is a behavioral loop of sin driven by shame, driven by sin, etc.—and I was in it. I had been in it for years. She was only stating the obvious.

Time has shown that she was wrong.

Forgiveness unlocked the door to a path of hope. And change.

SELAH: CHAPTER ONE

Have you ever felt trapped in a loop of sin and shame?

Can you identify with those feelings in an area of your life currently?

On a scale of one to ten, how much hope do you feel for change?

CHAPTER TWO

IT'S ALL ABOUT YOU

Lewis Smedes once stated, "When we forgive we set a prisoner free." He added, "Then we find out that the prisoner was us." Forgiveness is not about someone else. Forgiveness is about you. Regardless of the pain we have suffered and/or the justice that we feel should be exacted upon the perpetrator, withholding forgiveness only harms us. The act of forgiveness is far more freeing for the giver than it is for the receiver.

When I was a public school teacher I would see middle schoolers wearing t-shirts emblazoned with the slogan, "It's all about me." As adults, we laugh. We roll our eyes. We lecture, "Boy, is life gonna give you a wake-up call." But when it comes to the principles of forgiveness, I couldn't agree more. This book should come with a shirt that reads "It's all about me." We could market the slogan on t-shirts, golf shirts, crew necks, and cardigans. We could even offer a refrigerator magnet. A screensaver. Whatever it takes to change our thinking and remind us that giving forgiveness is all about me.

A decade of pastoral care has shown me that an unwillingness to forgive is, without question, the most common hurdle to growth and wellness in individuals and families. This observation holds true regardless of whether individuals identify as Christian or non-Christian. We all have our hurts. We all have been wounded by the happenings of life. Do a little soul searching and you'll identify people whom you have forgiven or whom you need to forgive. If you've been breathing for very long, it's a given that you've needed to do some forgivin'. My wife, Melinda, and I conservatively estimate that eight in ten of our pastoral care sessions ultimately touch upon the concepts of forgiveness as a key to effectively moving people toward growth and recovery. These forgiveness principles have become the focus of intervention in our ministry.

FUNCTIONAL NON-FORGIVERS

The irony is that there is no specific criminal profile for these "functional non-forgivers." I am convinced that most people (the unscientific eighty percent as stated above) are "functional non-forgivers." We're like the functional alcoholic. We go to work every day. Provide for the needs of our family and children. Go to holiday parties and Saturday picnics. We make sure our grass is mowed. We may even worship God and have His Spirit in our lives. Still, we are in need of forgiveness.

"But I didn't do anything," you say. "Why would I need forgiveness?"

This question reveals the very core of the issue.

The great majority of those eight in ten are not in need of receiving forgiveness . . . they are in need of giving forgiveness. The hours and energies we invest in these folks are not expended in helping them ask for forgiveness. The educational and spiritual work we offer is in helping them come to the place where they can give it.

Remember, it's all about you.

Forgiveness is all about you.

Many times professing, active Christians think that they are "all set" because they make a confession for Christ, receive His Spirit, and convert to a lifestyle of godly separation and holiness. They have been born again of water and Spirit. I rejoice with them, but this is an experience and it is only the beginning. It is being born again. These folks have been given Life—new Life with a capital "L." That is exactly what Jesus came for. But there is a deeper purpose—a progressive plan.

Jesus Himself expressed that there is a measurable distinction between "life" and "abundant life." He came to bring life, and that more abundantly (John 10:10 KJV). One translation (NIV) characterizes it as "life . . . to the full." I find this distinction played out every day in the lives of men and women, family and friends. We are alive, but we are not full. We are alive, but we are broken. We are breathing and active, but our legs are broken. We can move, but we can't walk. We may be able to walk, but we can't run. We have been born to new life, which is better than what we had, but we have not moved into the experience of the abundant life Jesus mentioned as being available. We are "functional non-forgivers."

There is an attainable realm of abundant living.

It is promised. It is available. It won't just happen.

Weeds just happen. And although some weeds host colorful flowers, they never produce any fruit. There is hope for contentment beyond just coping. There is hope for fullness instead of failure. But it won't just happen because you have the Holy Spirit any more than your broken leg will get fixed because you have a medical insurance card in your wallet! It is going to require some action from you and some action from the Great Physician. Unite with the Spirit of God and let the healing begin. It is a spiritual act that I believe has already begun. I believe God is involved in your life—right now—and I believe that you are closer to healing than when you first opened this book. You're not at a crossroad. You've already moved through that intersection and have begun to move along the path of promise. My prayer is that the next chapter opens your understanding to the dynamics of oppression and turns a light on for you that allows you to engage the power of the Spirit of God to still the voices of shame, fear, and sorrow in your life.

(I stopped typing and prayed the sentence above. I am asking you to do the same. We need a Higher Power to pull this off and it won't be fully successful without Him. Also, thanks for exercising the courage and making this journey with me. The freedom that lies ahead is phenomenal.)

Selah: ChapterTwo

When you think of forgiveness—do you think of yourself or others?

Do you think of forgiveness as an act of giving or receiving?

When you consider your walk with God, would you label it as life or abundant life?

Do you recognize that God is leading you toward more abundant living?

CHAPTER THREE

THE VOICES

L ast summer I was walking along the boardwalk at Venice Beach with my family and Los Angeles missionary Justin Frailey. It was a breezy afternoon and the crowd was light. As we strolled along, a young man walked past me and something caught my attention. It was his shirt—the message read, "Don't get mad at me, just because the voices don't talk to you!" He passed as quickly as he had approached. There was no verbal interaction or eye contact between us, but his silent message caused my mind and spirit to race into activity. I began to think about the voices.

His shirt was a comic spin on the pleas of temporary insanity that filter through our court systems and psychological assessment centers. "I heard a voice. Someone told me to . . ." Statements akin to "the devil made me do it." The comic value of this shirt's message would lead me to conclude that most people have come to scoff at the idea of voices telling us what to do or directly influencing our behaviors. We file these situations as pertaining to the mentally deranged or the demon possessed.

Most folks don't believe in the voices. I do.

In fact, I don't just believe in the existence of the voices. . . . I believe they talk to us. All of us. All the time. Acknowledging their presence in my life doesn't mean that I am mentally insane or demon possessed. It means I am human. It means I have an understanding that there are real-time spiritual influences. It means that I may have some unresolved issues that have made me vulnerable to their influence.

These influencers are voices of shame, fear, and sorrow.

For far too many, they are the background noise of a lifetime. They are the supermarket music of life— not really acknowledged, but always there. We hum a tune as we push our grocery cart across the parking lot. We sing the line to a song as we sit at a red light. We wonder where that song came from. It came from aisle five. You see, there was more going on in that store than just coupon cutting and comparison shopping. You were being influenced. Directed. Slightly manipulated.

SUPERMARKET PSYCHOLOGY

There is a psychology to our supermarket experience. The daily staples of milk, eggs, and bread are placed in the back corner of the store, ensuring that we pass everything else to get to them. Name brands are placed at eye level making it as easy as possible to pay more. Pleasant music plays softly and subtly. I know that, for some, this comparison is running the risk of the ridiculous, but it is an example that I can wrap my mind around. These subtle voices within the music get inside our heads and follow us out of the supermarket. They stay with us, but do not lie dormant. They affect our behavior and come out in the line of a song or the familiar tune that we hum walking across the parking lot.

Try it on yourself. Tomorrow morning when you get up, leave yourself a note to hum the first few bars of "Jingle Bells" or "Happy Birthday to You." Just do a couple of bars—five seconds or so. See if you're not humming it while you're dressing or eating breakfast or driving around later that morning. If you're not, chances are pretty good your spouse will be!

Shame, fear, and sorrow. The voices in aisle five. The voices in the parking lot. The voices at 2 A.M. The voices during the sermon.

News flash . . . forgiveness begins the process of stilling the voices. The Spirit closes the deal.

THE KINGDOM OF GOD IS . . .

The apostle Paul wrote to the church at Rome that "the kingdom of God is not eating and drinking, but righteousness and peace and joy in the Holy Spirit" (Romans 14:17 NKJV). This verse does not solely reference a future kingdom with streets of gold and gates of pearl where angels flitter from cloud to cloud. This promise of righteousness, peace, and joy in the Holy Spirit can be real-time, right now stuff. Although not apparently accessed by all, it is available to all. In fact, these three conditions or states of living seem to be the identifying characteristics of kingdom membership on this earth.

I was recently in a small group Bible study when the group identified peace, joy, happiness, and a better life as four desirable results of Christian living. After gaining consensus from the group that these were accurate, I asked, "On a scale of one to five, rate how you are doing in each of these areas. Has your walk with God automatically moved these ratings to 'five' status?" There were several sheepish grins and a few embarrassed eyebrow raises. Those looks told me what I already assumed to be true—people want to live in righteousness, peace, and joy, but something is keeping them from fullness. Jesus referred to this fullness as abundant life.

Again, Paul presented a corollary verse that offers the insight into how we can overcome the negative and access the positive. Second Timothy 1:7 states, "For God has not given us a spirit of fear, but of power and of love and of a sound mind" (NKJV).

We are supposed to live in righteousness, peace, and joy. Often we don't. God has, thankfully, given us the tools (implied as the spirit of power, the spirit of love, and the spirit of a sound mind) to address these shortfalls. There is a literal and ordered connection between these two verses: Romans 14:17 and II Timothy 1:7. When written side by side, they match like a pair of Christmas mittens and they join to lay the foundation for freedom and a fully realized spiritual life. Righteousness, identified first in Romans 14:17, is connected to a spirit of power, identified first in II Timothy 1:7. Secondly, peace is connected to a spirit of love. Joy, listed as the third promised characteristic, is connected to the spirit of a sound mind. It becomes a simple comparison of the desired components of each verse—first with first, second with second, and third with third. The freeing impact of the application is far from common.

STILL THE SHAME

Righteousness is noted first as a realm of daily living that we are to enjoy. To be righteous means to be just. To be just is to be innocent. To be justified means it is "just as if I" had never done it. Justification is beyond being found not guilty. It is an acquittal. The actions are expunged from your record. No one can find a trace of what was done and, as long as we practice forgiveness, we cannot be brought up on those specific charges again. That is truly free. It is the ultimate Presidential pardon. That is righteousness.

The absence of this righteousness may reveal the presence of shame. I am not feeling innocent. I am the woman at the well in John 4. I am full of shame and go to draw water in the heat of the day, the sixth hour, in order not to have to face my life choices and the scorn of the more acceptable women. I am at the well and I meet a Man. He asks me some questions. He shouldn't. He asks me to bring my husband. I am honest, but reticent. Nervous. Drawn out, but still guarded. I tell Him that I don't have one. Then it happens. He tells me what I have worked so hard to avoid. He knows that I am living with a man. He knows my sin and the sins of my past. This is the reason that I come to the well at noon—so I don't have to deal with this. So I don't have to hear about myself! I turn from His view and drop my head in shame. That's what we're talking about. The absence of a feeling of innocence can reveal the presence of shame.

These are the voices of our past. They are the voices of our shame. It is the voice of Satan to us. It is the voice of us to us. We have been promised a spirit of power to still the voice of Satan, but we have to forgive ourselves if we hope to close his door of entry and influence. When we have been wounded (self-inflicted or victimized) and then keep the wound alive and oozing, we give Satan a door of entry. The door has to be closed.

To accept the righteousness of God, we must first forgive ourselves. Satan is an accuser of the brethren. It is his job. He's not going to stop trying, but we can access a power to close the door to his influence. We are given a spirit of power to face our past—the hurting person that we were—and to forgive ourselves. That is who we were. It is an ugly picture, but it's not new news to God.

He knew us. He knows us. He has already accepted us. As is. He is the prodigal father who is extravagant and wasteful with His love to us. He is the prodigal father who puts a robe of righteousness around our filth and brokenness. He is the one who is prodigal because His behavior is abnormal and unexpected. His actions deviate from the norm. A wasteful young son and an angry good brother are not unexpected. Love, when scorned, and full acceptance, when betrayed, are unexpected responses. But they are God's responses and He is looking down the road of your return—ready to act them out for every one, every time.

The spirit of power will give you the strength and courage to accept His offer. It will give you the support to return to the Father—to be honest with yourself, your world, and your God. It will give you the power to forgive—to release your right to punish yourself for the rest of your life. We all make the mistakes. We all need the self-directed forgiveness. But we don't all access the spiritual power to do it. You can. It's a prayer away. Receive the spirit of power, forgive yourself, and still the voices of accusation. Accept the righteousness that He stands ready to bathe you in.

STILL THE FEAR

The absence of peace may reveal the presence of fear. We are not at ease. We have chilling moments of uncertainty about our salvation, our acceptance by God, and our love from Him. We question our "readiness" for the Rapture. Our ear has become deaf to the voices of shame, but what about God's ear? We know Satan accuses us to the Father. He did it to Job and we can't hope to be treated any differently. I don't know how he does it, but Satan approaches the presence of God and talks trash about us. He offers some not so subtle reminders to the omniscient One. Amazing.

Knowing this, we may be stricken with a fear that God might one day believe Satan's lobbying. We fear that the love that we thought was unconditional may not be. Satan is the father of lies, but we believe that these comments are true. We know that we really are as unworthy as Satan says and that fuels our fear. Peace evades us because we have this nagging belief that one day God will come to His senses and kick us out. That's not gonna happen. Jesus knew that Peter would deny Him and He still commissioned Peter to preach on the Day of Pentecost. Jesus knew the story of the woman at the well and He still gave her the revelation of the Living Water. Jesus Christ loves us and has provided a spirit of love to flow over us and wash away the fear of a Father's rejection—regardless of our experiences with our natural fathers. The spirit of love stills the voices of the present—voices that accuse us and cause us to doubt God's extensions of love. It brings the power to grow peace in our lives.

STILL THE SORROW

Our voice is strong. The voice of Satan can be strong. But the voice that can stay with us like a rock in our shoe—always irritating—always affecting our walk—is the voice of circumstances. Circumstances that will never change. We are promised joy, but circumstances strip us of joy and the void is filled with sorrow. My parents died when I was a teenager. They're not coming back. There is nothing I can do to change that. For years that circumstance was a constant wound. It was a constant sorrow. There was no room for joy because I was filled with sorrow. Jesus came to change that. The spirit of a sound mind offers an alternative.

GOD'S PART—OUR PART

We need the power of the Spirit. I echo the question of the great apostle in Galatians 3:3—will we ever be perfected in the flesh? The rhetorical question is answered with a resounding "No." It is a co-op. In the way I get my mind around it . . . we fight spirit with Spirit. As a human, I am certainly no match for demonic power. I understand that those battles are "out-of-body" experiences that occur in a supernatural zone. The door of entry . . . now that I can handle. The issue is one of Satan's power and Satan's influence. The Spirit of God deals with demonic power. You and I deal with demonic influence. We'll look at this in-depth in chapter seven, but know for now that we close the door of influence through our forgiveness. We do. We hold the key to our freedom. We do. In this respect, it is all about you.

Forgiveness, with the power of God's Spirit, stills the voices. They may not always be completely removed, in the case of an unchangeable life circumstance, but our ear can be shut to their accusations and Satan's "foothold" in our life (Ephesians 4:27 NIV) can be removed. This situation reminds me of the age-old question . . . if a tree falls in the forest and no one is around to hear it, does it make a sound? Sound waves are certainly produced but if there is no receptor (or ear) to convert the energy wave to actual sound, then there is no sound. There is certainly nothing to receive it.

NO MORE BUTTONS

I immediately think of Jesus' statement to his disciples near the end of His earthly ministry. Jesus related a life event and revealed a life condition when He said, "Hereafter I will not talk much with you: for the prince of this world cometh, and hath nothing in me" (John 14:30 KJV). The NIV reads that "the prince of this world . . . has no hold on me." Isn't that awesome? Isn't that so encouraging? Jesus Christ didn't have any buttons! Satan could holler and accuse and rail on and on and on, but it had no effect on our Savior. Jesus had lived a life of suffering and trial, just like we do, but He effectively dealt with the hurts and the shame through forgiveness. Chapter eight more effectively addresses how He did it, but I wanted to give you some hope to keep reading. It happened for Him and it can happen for us.

Chapter one is entitled "Hope for a Change." Chapter three will end with the same statement to you. Keep reading, friend. There is hope . . . for a change . . . in you.

SELAH: CHAPTER THREE

Identify your understanding, comfort level, and experience concerning negative spiritual influences.

Can you identify any unresolved issues of shame, fear, and/or sorrow that would cause you to be vulnerable to their destructive influence?

On a scale of one to five how are you doing in the areas of experiencing righteousness, peace, and joy in the Holy Ghost?

What are your buttons? Who are the button pushers?

CHAPTER FOUR

COMMON GROUND

The Gospels of Matthew, Mark, and Luke tell a story about soils. It is actually a parable and is often identified as the parable of the sower. I think the story is way more revealing about the condition of the soil than the sower.

WE'VE GOT 'EM ALL

The parable opens with a man taking a handful of seed and casting it onto the soil. The story then addresses the various conditions of ground upon which the seed fell. One area was thorny. Another stony. A third was labeled good ground and the last was distinguished as being by the wayside.

This parable is somewhat unique in that Jesus identified the typology of each soil. The thorny ground symbolized the cares of life that would choke out the seed and steal its ability to mature. The stony ground represented blocks to growth that would allow quick, but shallow, growth. The good ground was distinguished even further as soil that produced at different levels—some thirty-fold, some sixty-fold, and some one hundred-fold. And finally, the wayside ground was an area where the birds (identified as the devil) would come and devour the seed before it had time to take root and grow.

Jesus revealed the typology, but a new convert unlocked the application for me. I was a young home missionary pastor and we were hosting a Bible study in our home. I was feeding the lambs and waxing eloquently about this parable when one of our recent converts asked, "Do you think we are only one of these?"

After clearing my throat and glancing to the others, I choked out a "Well, yes."

Now this may be a "duh" insight to you, but it was revelatory for me. She clarified her point by stating that we are not one of four, but we possess all four types of ground simultaneously. I quickly realized it was true and it opened a window of application for me for which I will be forever grateful.

I've got 'em all. Even though I am a believer in Jesus? . . . yes. Even though I am an ordained minister and a pastor? . . . yes. Even though I have the Holy Spirit? . . . yes. Even though I am used by God in spiritual gifts? . . . yes. They're all there.

Some might argue the point, but consider the following:

The thorns represent the cares of life. Do you have a mailbox? Then you probably are in touch with the cares of life.

The wayside ground represents the devil's attempts to steal the seed that was meant to bear fruit in our lives. Has the devil bothered you lately?

How about the good ground? Don't you have some areas of your life that are going really well? You're producing God fruit. Some parts are good. Others better. And some are the best. This is just like a harvest that is thirty-fold, sixty-fold, or one hundred-fold.

My premise is this . . . if we have these three existing together, then we certainly have the fourth up and running in our lives. The stony ground.

Are there any areas where you feel blocked? You know what I mean. The seed shoots up fast on Sunday, but withers when the sun of Tuesday afternoon hits it. The reason lies in the fact that this new and burgeoning growth cannot get to water. Mark's account (4:5) states that there was "no depth of earth" while Luke's account (8:6) states that it "lacked moisture." Lacking depth? Feeling dry? The problem is a stone. A block.

But the real problem is that we can categorically deny the presence of stones in our lives because they are under the surface. They are unseen. The mailbox we can see. Satan we just accept. The stone? That's another story. Unfortunately it happens to be a part of the same story. The same story that is told in Matthew, Mark, Luke, my life, and your life. Stones are part of the story.

A CRITICAL UNDERSTANDING

It is vital that we get this. The process of creating stones will be detailed in chapter seven. The objective right now is to entertain and accept the idea that you may have some. We can live a life where we don't have any—Jesus did—but most of the folks I know, myself included, aren't there yet.

Giving first-time consideration is a huge step toward healing and freedom. You know what they say . . . "denial" is not just a river in Egypt. We will never address what we refuse to acknowledge. Satan's only strength is deception. A child of God is equipped through the Spirit of God to be greater than he that is in the world, but we won't fight what's not there. Or at least what we don't acknowledge as being there. Satan's strength of warfare is that many times we don't exercise spiritual discernment and flush him out. He wreaks havoc unchecked. If he can get us to deny the presence of stones in our hearts, he can keep our spiritual man stunted, frustrated, and immature. He would love nothing more.

This is where so many Spirit-filled Christians find themselves. They have received the Holy Spirit. They are faithful attendees to church activities. They love God and honor Him with their time, their treasures, and their talents. They have Life (with a capital "L"). The problem is . . . they have a broken leg. A wounded heart. A clouded mind. Stones are not often an issue of sin, but an issue of growth. It is not about life, but abundant life. Please remember that.

This book is not about labeling anyone or heaping hot coals of guilt on any heads. Jesus is not about that and I'm not either. This book, as a tool of the Spirit of God, will turn the light on Satan's deception and our denial. Don't worry about judgment from me. In the next chapter you will get a look at my story. A story that qualifies me to be the poster boy for shame and denial. God healed me. Little by little. Forgiveness after forgiveness. Step by step. He walked with me and gave me the personal courage and external support to face the music and do the work. The same thing can happen to you. It will require trust, time, and some tears. But a turn is in your future.

SELAH: CHAPTER FOUR

How do you feel about the fact that you may have stones?

What are the areas of your life that are really productive?

What areas in your life struggle to gain consistency?

CHAPTER FIVE

MY STORY—PART ONE

I was a good kid. The problem is that "bad" things happen to "good" people. It rains on the just and on the unjust. Hurt is headed your way and offenses are coming. The death angel of the Exodus story would pass over some houses and visit others. Pain doesn't abide by those parameters. Unlike the death angel of Egypt, pain is going to touch us all— blood covered or not.

THE MENTAL GAME

Often our suppression of pain is facilitated by our ability to rationalize and compartmentalize the situation. Our analytical Western mind reviews the painful situation, dissects its contributing parts, labels each by percentage of effect, slaps them in a mental folder, and then files them in the archives of our life. We find ourselves thinking: "It doesn't make sense to grieve. I can't do anything to change it. They didn't do it on purpose. That's water under the bridge. Can't cry over spilled milk" . . . or a number of other not-so-helpful hand-me-down Americanisms. When socialized in a culture of self-made men and women, what doesn't make sense or those things out of my control are ridiculous to even address. The mental game is an emotional disconnect. You don't have to have a college degree to effectively execute these mental gymnastics. I performed them flawlessly as a seventeen-year-old. A perfect ten.

As the youngest of four and the child of older parents, I was my mother's sunshine. I was the joker—the high achiever with the sense of humor. I had no idea how well this would play into my proficiency at dodging the pain. School was a breeze for me. I always seemed to finish my daily assignments during school hours and rarely had homework. Throughout grade school and high school I never earned a final grade lower than an A. It just wasn't that much of a challenge for me. I played music since the fourth grade and performed using brass, woodwinds, keyboards, and drums. I started varsity baseball as a freshman. I was the editor of the school paper. I was active and deeply connected to our church youth group. I thought I was fearless and flawless.

I thought.

Fortunately, yes, fortunately, I was wrong. (Of course you already knew that, didn't you?)

Mentally, emotionally, socially, and physically I was pretty solid—acknowledged nationally as being a teenager at the top of his game. Still, I had a flaw at a fundamental place. It was in the fifth component of holistic wellness—my spirit. The SAT didn't test for that. I had a relationship with the church, but not with God. It was professional, but not personal. Essentially, I was connected to the community of believers. It felt like being connected to God, but it wasn't. It was close, but not a ringer. It couldn't even be considered a leaner. I had a relationship with Bethel (the house of God), but not with El-Bethel (the God of the house of God). That was fixin' to change. God was about to start getting very personal.

THE SEVENTEENTH SUMMER

My mother had been battling a rare form of cancer for several years. As I recall, my mother was told that only a half-dozen women had this type. They had all died.

It was during the middle of my high school years when the cancer began to take a visible toll on Mom. Her body became more and more frail, while her spirit grew more grounded. She consumed the Word of God. I don't think a day would pass without Mom showing me something that she had read that day in the Scriptures. It was her lifeline.

I recall a particular Sunday night in April when my dad had to help Mom step onto a single step to enter the church. She was too weak to lift her foot the required five or six inches. I can see that interchange like it happened yesterday. The choir, of which I was a part, sang that night. During one of the songs, my mom shot out of her seat like someone had placed an explosive charge under her pew. My jaw dropped open.

49

I stopped singing. I couldn't believe what I had just witnessed. You can probably envision the few frames of the story—that Pentecostal church went nuts. A great faith hit that room and people were in the aisles worshiping God, praying for each other, and dancing before the Lord. Tremendous exuberance and expectation were evident. An old-fashioned prayer line formed and I think everyone in the church building went through it. Mom was last.

IT'S GOING TO BE ALL RIGHT

After she received prayer, mom began to twirl and laugh. She was absolutely fluid in her movements. Holy Ghost waltzing, as I've come to call it. It was beautiful. While this was happening a saint began to give a message in tongues and another trusted saint of God gave the interpretation. Several things were said, but the phrase that caught my attention was, "everything is going to be all right." That was my cue—*I* went nuts. I grabbed the hands of my great-aunt (eighty years of age at the time) and we danced in a circle. Smiling and laughing and thanking God. "Everything is going to be all right" meant that mom would be healed. Nine weeks later we buried her.

My family was a wreck. Mom was the first near relative to pass away in over twenty years. Family swarmed our house. It was during this chaos of care that I stepped into my bedroom and shut the door. I remember sitting on the edge of the bed and reaching for my Bible.

We lived two blocks from my high school and for

those past two years my mother had met me almost every day, most often during lunch, with a verse of Scripture that she had encountered that day. The Word of God was her lifeline. Her hunger for it was voracious. Little by little, she transmitted her passion and its power to me. I didn't even know it was happening. Until that day. I sat on the edge of the bed and clutched the very thing that she promised would stand infallible forever. I recall my words to be, "She said this would work. Prove it." It wasn't really an imperative statement from an arrogant teen, but more of a desperate prayer from a spiraling kid. I held the spine of the Bible and let it fall open. The pages parted near the middle—in the Book of the Psalms. My eyes were drawn to the left as several words seemed to elevate from the page. "I will lift up mine eyes unto the hills, from whence cometh my help. My help cometh from the LORD." It was the 121st psalm. It was God's Word . . . to me. I whispered a "thank you" and closed the cover. Like a car merging into traffic, I opened the bedroom door and walked back into my new world.

ROUND TWO

Some amazing things happened to comfort me during the following days. (Only the Lord knew how I was going to need it.) I found out that my mother passed just after praying with our pastor in the hospital. In fact, he told me that she worshiped and prayed wonderfully during that late morning prayer. When he concluded with the words, "In Jesus' name, amen," he opened his eyes and she was gone. The God-message spoken in our church in April and His words to me from Psalm 121 were becoming the foundation of ongoing comfort for me. Then as we stood at the grave site, God again offered His expression of love. The moment Pastor Eskridge opened the Bible and began to speak—rain began to pour down upon the green spring grass. He spoke but I could not hear his words. The tears of heaven drowned them out. These soaking rains ended the moment that he stopped speaking and tucked his Bible under his arm. It sounds bizarre. Even melodramatic. But that's exactly how it happened. The full force of the loss had not hit me yet, but I knew God was involved and aware of my life. The Creator of the universe had His eyes on me.

Nineteen days later I walked into my house and found my dad slumped over in his chair. I recognized the pallor of his skin and I knew he was dead. With the greatest of calm and self-assurance, I went to the phone and made the appropriate calls: 911, the pastor, and my sister-in-law. I walked back into the living room where my dad sat and waited for the circus to start. As I stood next to him, my eyes lifted and I saw my reflection in a large gilded mirror. A tremor of rage swelled from my chest and I thought of kicking the heavy wooden entry door from its hinges. It was a flash of a second. Barely visible to the natural eye. I did not act on the anger. I tactfully, and with poise, suppressed it. Little did I know how gifted I would be at the art of suppression. Little did I know how much depravation it would induce.

Here we go again. Three weeks later I am sitting in

the same room with the same question. I don't remember having my Bible, but I do remember my prayer. "Now what? How do You top that?" (Referencing His divine intervention nineteen days earlier.)

It wasn't a moment until I heard the words in my head, "Where was My father when I died?"

Now, I had grown up in the church and attended Sunday school every week of my life. I knew the Bible. I knew the stories. I was well taught, so I started my hard drive and scanned the Gospel accounts of the Crucifixion. I knew Jesus was there. I knew Mary was there. I knew John was there. But there was no mention of Joseph. I knew husbands were often a decade or more older than their brides. I knew that Jesus had given the care of His mother to John. He officially connected them as mother and son. No Joseph.

My response to this history lesson was simply, "He wasn't there, Lord." And His response to me was, "I know what it's like to lose a dad." Again, miraculous.

What can you say? The pain doesn't go away. Truth be told, it hadn't even really started yet. But I knew He was there. He wanted me to remember and I never forgot.

The Cream of the Cream

I moved in with my brother and sister-in-law. Steve and Sara gave me guidance and care. They loved me and made great sacrifices to welcome me and deal with the baggage I was picking up along the way. I graduated from high school and went to college. I had applied to the United States Naval Academy in Annapolis, Maryland, and attended a junior college in the fall and a Bible school in the spring while I awaited the Academy's decision.

I took the oath as a midshipman on July 1, 1987, and poured myself into the discipline and military rigors of such an institution. I excelled and quickly rose to the top of my class. By my senior year, I was a battalion commander—in the top ten (of 4,500) militarily—with the ceremonial oversight of over 750 young men and women. I was the cream of the crop among the cream of the crop. Pretty heady stuff for a twenty-two-year-old. Fairly easy to do when you're driven by anger and shame. Being shut down to your emotions and the emotions of others can be quite valuable in the short run of self-promotion.

The untold story was that I would walk around with an inferno of anger just beneath a membrane-thick skin. I recall a specific day in the spring. The flowers were gorgeous—the tulips planted in rows of red and yellow. The warm sun glistened from the massive windows of academic buildings and a soft, salty breeze blew in from the bay. These were the days when the anger was the nearest. Kenny Chesney sings about it when he reflects, "Sunny days seem to hurt the most. I wear the pain like a heavy coat. I just can't believe you're gone."

It was in the most beautiful days when I felt the emptiness most profoundly. I wanted my dad to be there. I wanted him to see me. I wanted him to be proud of his son. It would never happen. He would never know. This realization made me a walking time bomb. Had an innocent bystander bumped against me during one of these reflective episodes, I know that I could have easily harmed him. "Harmed him" is the soft version. The thoughts that came to me were heartless and brutal. I was suffering and I didn't have too much concern for the suffering of anyone else. In fact, inflicting a little here and there—sharing the wealth—seemed fair to me.

6 2 4 7 1 3

These emotions and reactions were not the problem. They were a by-product. The problem was that I was not dealing with the impact of the pain or the offense from my loss. The only work I did around my parents' deaths was to keep the wound alive. I thought of it as "memorializing" them, but it was really just picking at the scab to ensure that the wound stayed fresh. A lot of people do this same thing.

One day my roommate was checking my email for me while I was cleaning up to go out. He asked for my password and I told him, "624713." He inquired about the meaning of that number. I tried to dodge the question. I told him that he didn't really want to know. He kept at it, refusing to let it go. (As you'll see, I guess that made two of us!) Finally I explained that "624" is for June 24 and "713" is for July 13—the days that my parents died. His reaction was shock, embarrassment, and sadness—more for me than for himself, I think.

It wasn't until years later that I realized those

numbers played a strategic role in my shame. They were constant reminders of my pain. And they were chosen. They were specifically placed, by me, in my daily life so that I would have to reconnect to the loss with every log-on I made. That's not memorializing. That is picking at the scab.

I don't know exactly where the line is, but there is one. It is the line that we cross when our grieving transforms into self-inflicted wounding.

> The tragedy happened once.
>> The parent or child died once.
> The breakup happened once.
>> The abuse or rejection happened once.

Our choice to place reminders throughout our daily life causes the wounding to happen again and again and again.

These wounds are self-inflicted. Maybe we're punishing ourselves. Maybe we just don't realize what we are doing. Either way, it must stop if healing can ever fully be realized in your life. Wounds that stay open get infected and there is nothing pretty about that.

SELAH: CHAPTER FIVE

Have you found God to be as real as He was to me?

Remember the times when He has "spoken" to you and reconnect with how much He cares for you.

When you consider the hurts in your life, are you "memorializing" them or "picking the scab"?

CHAPTER SIX

DOOR NUMBER ONE

I remember watching "Let's Make a Deal" as a young child. Monty Hall's famous phrasing still rings in my mind . . . "Is it behind door number one, or door number two, or door number three?" I don't really remember anything else about the show. I just remember his repeated question and those doors with the large numbers.

Just weeks after my graduation and commissioning as a naval officer, God chose to show what was behind Door Number One in my life. I actually knew we were in the game. I just didn't know when the door would be opened.

I had just recommitted my life to Jesus Christ with no expectations and no strings attached. I was a broken young man who knew I needed Him if I ever hoped to find freedom and healing. Relationships had been disconnected. (Severing might be more applicable in some cases.) I felt as if I were starting over. In truth, I was just starting.

Over the previous two weeks my pastor and I had

begun to discuss my need for inner healing. I was living in his home for the summer and that afforded us ample time to sit together and talk. Free time was something I definitely had—my closest friendships had been shelved.

Insanity is doing the same thing you've always done and expecting different results. Well, I had tried to live for God on numerous occasions in the past and failed. It seemed like I was on and off every other week. I had friends back home who would kid with me, "Are we in the two weeks 'on' or the two weeks 'off'? Are you going to be handing out tracts or should we buy beer?" I know they were joking around, but their observations were telling of my internal struggles.

The secular connections were too strong to overcome with my limited level of commitment to God. Some fault was theirs. Some of it was mine. Either way, I couldn't break the cycles of behavior. I couldn't break the habits. My current choices were extreme, but extreme was what my situation demanded. History had proven that I couldn't break free from the behaviors of sin (review chapter one).

He and I researched the influences, the causes, the effects. We were both trained as engineers and we discussed my healing with the candid tones of corporate problem solvers. There were no tears or breakout prayer sessions. We simply discussed the issues. Emotions seemed to be disconnected in me. It was as if I was trouble-shooting the circuitry of someone else's life. Until Sunday night.

The church seated about 750 people that night. I sat in the back row on the aisle. It's been over fifteen years since that night and I can see it like it happened this morning. Pastor Wright finished his message, prayed for a few folks, and made his way down the long aisle to where I stood. His question was simple and direct—similar to the tone of our previous interactions.

"Are you ready to do this?" I nodded a yes. He swept his arm in the direction of the altar and, with a slight smile, moved across the back of the church to pray with other people.

All right. So this is how it is, I thought. No fanfare here. Just me and God and a long walk to the front. I stood at the altar—a singular figure—and waited. My eyes were closed as I gave the Lord my okay to begin. It seemed as if a minute passed before it happened. The Great Physician had donned his scrubs and was opening Door Number One.

I never really saw it coming. At least not in the magnitude that hit me. One instant I was standing still, composed and compliant. The next immediate instant I was sobbing and doubled forward. It was like a switch had been thrown. I guess it was the switch that turned the light on behind the door.

There were three visions/images that played from the projector of my mind. I don't fully remember the first or the third, but I can still visualize the second. I approached a large wooden door with a small observation window above the push plate. It was the door to a hospital room. As I opened it and looked in, I saw a young woman sitting up in the hospital bed with a newborn in her arms. The woman was my longtime love and the baby was mine. When this picture flashed across my mind, I again doubled over and the sobbing became uncontrollable.

It happened like this three distinct times.

I would bend forward, as if struck in the back of the head, and heave and cry. It doesn't sound too pretty . . . and it wasn't. My shoulders would shake as if I had heard a hilarious joke. Unfortunately I wasn't laughing. I was crying. In fact the fluids were running from my eyes, nose, and mouth like the proverbial faucet. These reactions seemed to be controlled from somewhere else because they would stop as quickly as they started. One. Two. Three. No one prayed with me. It was the Master and I.

After the third episode, I looked up to the platform and saw Pastor Wright standing behind the pulpit. I was okay. It was a somewhat surreal moment, but I knew I had come through something. I didn't feel the victory of a conqueror or the despair of the vanquished. I remember just breathing. I stood there breathing, taking inventory, like a crash victim who sits still behind the wheel and considers his condition. I felt accomplishment. Something had happened. Something I was trusting as good.

As I cleaned my face, I looked for an insight and softly asked, "Is that it? Is it over?" He looked at me with the eyes of a father and said, "I think so."

I didn't know what had happened. Although I don't recall the specifics of the other two visualizations, I do remember that they were equally painful to release.

It felt like I was living an episode from *A Christmas Carol*. A dream, a lifelong expectation, was wrapped in each vision. They were dreams that I once believed would become reality. They were dreams that I now knew would never be fulfilled. These were the dreams that had defined my identity. They were the pages of my life—the life that I had always planned for. The way I had always seen myself. Their chapters had been removed from the new book. Torn away, and it hurt.

In the moments that followed I stood there with my eyes closed. One by one the three scenes again passed across my mind. Nothing. I felt nothing. The surface of my soul didn't have a ripple. It was like an instant replay of the exact same visions being projected before the eyes of a different man. At the time, I didn't fully realize that our emotional reactions are such a tell-tale sign of healing. I didn't have any. God had done an instant healing. Wrenching, but instant. I *was* that different man.

I was thankful for God's involvement. I knew He was the Author of whatever it was that had just occurred. I felt okay. Actually proud—with the pride of a survivor. Too bad I didn't know that this was simply a pre-op procedure. Jesus was going for total healing.

Springtime in Annapolis can't be beat. Springtime in Annapolis, when it is your senior year at the Academy, is off the charts. You are da man. Free beers from people you've never met and kisses from girls you don't know. All you have to do is walk through the inner harbor in your dress whites with the stripes of a first class midshipman and renown comes a callin'. Again, really heady stuff for a twenty-three-year-old. This was the backdrop for the next Doctor's visit.

My family had come to Annapolis for my graduation and the week of ceremony and festivity that pre-
ceded it. The afternoon before the graduation found me
at my now ex-girlfriend's house. My family had been
connected with her for the previous seven years and, bro-
ken-up or not, they wanted to see her. My track record
proved that this God shift was just a momentary hiatus
and she and I would be back together soon enough.

They were visiting and catching up in the basement family room when she ran upstairs to get some
lemonade and refreshments. I followed. This was the
girl whom I loved. Our lives were more than connected. They were fused together. She was the reservoir
into which I poured all of my emotion following my
parents' deaths. Couple the intensity of that with our
sexual intimacy and we had a weld stronger than the
steel it connects.

She turned from the counter and I hugged her. I
held her and began to cry—not exactly feeling the
power of an overcoming Christian life. I was standing
in that kitchen with my past in hand and my destiny
fading fast. It was a crossroad. For me, in retrospect, it
might have been *the* crossroad.

I had broken up with her five weeks earlier and
now I was breaking in half. Emotion flooded my mind.
In that moment, I felt more alone than ever before. It
was more than releasing a girlfriend. It was more than
the loss of a singular relationship. She embodied my
identity. I didn't really know who I was or what I
would look like without her and the life we lived
together. For the past five weeks of my new life I had

seen two sets of footprints—mine and God's. Now I saw only one set. I thought they were mine. I thought I was facing a full, frontal assault from hell—alone. I was wrong. Not about the one set of footprints, just about Whose they were.

I released my embrace, wiped my eyes, and offered a broken, but sincere, apology. I didn't return to the basement. I found the keys to my Jeep and limped back to the pastor's home. My story of change was being written and God had just finished writing a new chapter.

The next day was my graduation. We had to be up before the birds in order to prepare and arrive for the formation and march-on. Pastor Wright was up and met me on the steps. He had prepared for the same ceremony twenty-three years earlier. After we shared some sentimental comments he asked how yesterday had gone. I could easily say that it was the roughest day so far.

I told my story.

Then he told God's story.

Pastor Wright was in the process of building a new home. They were in the planning stages and he would often drive around the community taking pictures of architectural designs that caught his attention. He was on one of these drives the previous day. As he was racing down the highway the Lord told him to pull over and pray for Andy. That was the exact quote . . . "Pull over and pray for Andy." There was not a convenient place to stop or turn so Pastor Wright responded that he would in a moment. God's reply was imperative, "Pull over now." He did and he prayed.

Pastor Wright asked me to remember the time of the "kitchen crossroad" with my ex. It was the same time. God directed my pastor to intercede for me during the very moment of my greatest growth challenge. Hell was coming in like a flood and, true to His Word, the Lord raised up a wall against it.

I could have passed on telling this story, but it would have been a disservice to you.

I am not special—at least not any more special to God than you are. He is no respecter of persons. When you return from your trip to the Great Physician, you will be hurting and vulnerable. That's the nature of surgery. It's the nature of healing. Satan may try to kick you while you're down—attack you during the recovery time. You're still trying to heal and he's throwing everything at his disposal. Old relationships. Dreams. Insecurities. Old habits. These will be the things within an arm's reach. You may have your arms around them, as I did. Please remember what I didn't know at the time. Somebody's praying for you. He or she is bridging the gap and providing a pathway to bring you to victory. God is fighting for you. Probably even while you're reading this book.

SELAH: CHAPTER SIX

Are you ready for God to reveal what is behind Door Number One in your life?

What emotion do you feel when you think about the possibility of this happening?

You don't have to wait for God to tell them. Whom can you contact who will pray for you as you move through the crossroads of your life?

CHAPTERSEVEN

THE INVITATION

Stones act as hinges and connect a door to your heart. A door that shuts God out. A door that lets Satan in. Stones often, if not always, reveal the presence of an initial wounding and a subsequent resentment. They result from a mishandled (non-biblically-handled) offense. The issue is not the presence of offense. Stones are introduced into our soil based upon how we handle the offense. These "stones" are more than just an abstract from an ancient parable. They exist in our physical world. Many of us already have some exposure to the natural process.

CLEARING THE LAND

The physical realm reflects the principles of the spiritual. Natural happenings provide the practical examples that help us connect our experience to a spiritual dynamic and process it. This is why Jesus taught from parables based upon situations in the natural world—a birth, a fishing net, living water, a seed, a tree, a treasure. Oh, and . . . stones.

We can get any travel guide or go online to see the monuments that reveal the stone principle to which Jesus referred. These monuments are fences. They adorn the New England landscape and are valued as architectural distinctives. Pastoring in Rhode Island afforded us the opportunity to see them on a daily basis. These two-foot-tall fences are made of flat stones. Field stones.

Although the fences are currently sought for decorative value, their history is far more practical. Landowners needed to grow crops. The New England landscape was stony ground. The stones were blocking the roots from going deep and reaching existing water sources. The landowners had to extract the stones if they hoped to enjoy a successful harvest. Once the stones were removed, they needed to be utilized. They were found to be useful as fences. The very things that inhibited growth, when removed and processed, now protected it. That sounds like a God-thing to me and that's where we're heading.

A HOOK TO HANG HIS HAT ON

Ephesians 4 gives us the insight into how we actually have invited the devil into our lives. Verse twenty-six reads, "Be angry, and do not sin: do not let the sun go down on your wrath" (NKJV). We are allowed to be angry. It is an emotion. It is a God-given emotion. Anger is not the problem. Sin is the problem. We are allowed to be angry but we are not allowed to sin.

So . . . how do we identify the line where anger transforms from an emotion to a sin?

The next phrase in Ephesians 4 answers that question: "do not let the sun go down on your wrath." Simple. We can't go to bed angry. Oh, boy . . . I'm figuring that's happened to you a night or two . . . huh? I don't think I'm going out on a limb here . . . it's happened to us all. I often joke around and encourage folks just to make sure they get angry in the morning! That being said, I don't think the issue is purely defined by the sunset. I certainly don't want to be errant with my theology, but for the sake of universal application, let's just call it a day—twenty-four hours. In this light, the ASV (Andy Smith Version) would read, "It's okay to be angry, but you're not allowed to sin. And by the way . . . you can't be angry for more than a day."

I can hear the peanut gallery now: "Okay, fine. All right already. I get it. I need to let go of the anger in a day or it's a sin. I don't want to sin, but I sin most days anyway. I'll just repent of this one like I repent of the others. Surely you didn't write a book with this as the cornerstone. Did you?"

I did.

I did because there is more to the story. In fact there is more to the sentence. Remember . . . the one we just read in Ephesians 4? We read verse twenty-six. Well, there is a verse twenty-seven and it doesn't just follow numerically. It is the end of the original sentence. The whole thing reads like this: (26) "Be angry, and do not sin: do not let the sun go down on your wrath, (27) nor give place to the devil" (NKJV). The NIV translates it by saying, "do not give the devil a foothold." Herein is the seriousness of the situation. Here is the invitation: "Come on in, devil. Can I take your hat and coat?"

So the answer is simple—just let go of the anger. Oh, how we all wish the act were that easy. Of course we know what to do, but the players in the drama of life don't always cooperate. Some of those players being ourselves. We're not just leveling a shovel into the ground and removing an inanimate object. The ground is our heart and the blade of the shovel hurts.

SMOOTHING THINGS OVER

The whole issue is about pain and our effectiveness or ineffectiveness at dealing with it from a biblical perspective.

We are like the oysters. (Again a natural example of a spiritual phenomenon.) An oyster is out there minding his own business when life places a grain of sand in his shell. It is just a grain of sand. Insignificant except for the fact that it lodged in the oyster's most tender place. The shell is hard. The exterior is covered. But that tender, pink inside is vulnerable and not really suited for this situation. The oyster chooses to coat the irritant with a milky coating. At last the sharp pain is gone. Unfortunately it is replaced by a different type of irritation. The edge is gone, but now the irritant, although smoother, is bigger. Well, the oyster will do what it's always done . . . coat it again. And again. And again. Too bad it never takes care of the problem. As humans, we understand the plight of the oyster and exploit it. Gals all around the world have beautiful pearl jewelry—thanks to Mr. Oyster.

We do the same thing. We cover the pain. We coat the irritation. We bury the wound. Deeper and deeper. It doesn't have the edge that it did, but it doesn't go away either. We're not trying to hurt ourselves or invite the devil into our lives. Truth be told, we are just trying to cope with the pain, keep functioning, and survive the unwanted situation. I understand. I think God does, too.

THE ADDICTION ANSWER

So many folks just don't know what to do with the pain of life. The offenses that we didn't ask for. The abuses that we didn't deserve. But we've got them so we have to deal with them. That's what every word on every page of this book is about. Drugs won't work. Sexual partners won't work. Throwing yourself into your career, although more socially acceptable, won't work either. The only value these have, in my mind, is that they have kept you going until you can get to a place where God can be personally involved. I have often told people, "Your drug use was not the best decision, but given your circumstances, it has kept you in the game until you could get to a pastor and begin to receive the help you need from God and the church." God can restore you. He can heal you.

The beautiful part is that you are seventy-seven pages closer to your healing. I know this because the

Great Physician never does surgery unless you are ready. I should say, unless He knows you're ready. You may not think you are right now, but, at some level, God must. (Remember, I talked to my pastor for a couple of weeks before God performed a demonstrative healing in me. The process that prepared me for that moment happened weeks earlier.) God will be caring to you. He will take everything into consideration and make sure you have what it is going to take.

When an elderly relative needs a surgical procedure, any competent physician will ensure that the patient is strong enough to survive the surgery. If not, the surgery will be postponed until he or she is. Doctors are concerned and attentive to ensure that patients survive the procedure. God is too. After all, He is not just a really good physician. He is the Great Physician. Trust Him with this.

BACK TO THE CLASSROOM

The process of offense is really not that hard to follow—especially considering that we've all had numerous opportunities to live it. We, like the oyster, are minding our own business. We could be five or fifty-five. Someone hurts us and we get wounded. We get angry. Enter Ephesians 4. It is at this point that we are met with a decision. Do we forgive or do we choose not to forgive? Those are the options and they are the only options. Aside from the fact that you have 1,440 minutes to do it . . . those are still the only options.

CANCER OF THE SOUL

Here's the rub. Sin hasn't happened yet and the devil hasn't been invited in yet. These possible outcomes really hinge on this decision. To forgive or not to forgive—that is the question. Can it be that easy? Well, it can be, but our emotions and expectations throw a wrench into the mix.

Check out this example: During one of our ministry sessions, a woman makes a comment about my bald head and several members of the audience begin to snicker. After the session, this woman approaches me and asks me to forgive her. I do. In fact it would be no problem for me to forgive her. I might wonder what her issues are, but I'd easily grant my forgiveness.

Now let's alter the situation slightly for day two. Same setting, same comment, same snickering, except this time the woman is my wife. On the ride home she asks me to forgive her. Hmmm. Start the clock—I understand that I have twenty-four hours to think about this! Seriously, I would not be as quick to forgive. I wouldn't even be as quick to consider forgiving. Why? What is the difference between the two situations? They were the same place, the same words, and the same response. The only difference was who said it. I had no relationship with the first woman and I have pledged my life in relationship to the second. Emotions and expectations are different and they make it more difficult to choose to forgive.

Consideration of this simple scenario brings great clarity to the dynamics of offense. When someone hurts me, I have a window of time to forgive him. If I don't forgive him, then it reveals the presence of resentment. I am not wounded by *what* was said as much as I am wounded by *who* said it. Does this clear up why we are hurt most by the ones we love? In effect it is resentment that blocks the choice of forgiveness. Forgiveness would come easily if resentment was not standing in its way. Resentment, unfortunately, is the seedling of a grudge. And a grudge is the sapling of bitterness. Bitterness is the cancer of the soul. Does that sound like a stone to you? Stones are the hurts that we bury, the wounds that we cover up, the offenses that we refuse to forgive. They block our growth and ensure that the life we do have begins to wither.

FREEDOM THROUGH FORGIVENESS

We, as individuals, hold the key for ourselves. It really is the key of freedom through forgiveness. In this context, we can be our own worst enemies. Of course, the wounding wasn't our fault, but the subsequent hardening of our hearts will be. Satan is more than happy to suck the life from us, but he is not totally at fault either. After all, we gave him the foothold through our unwillingness to forgive.

Paul gave sage wisdom when he highlighted this principle for his protégé, Timothy:

> *And the servant of the Lord must not strive; but be gentle unto all men, apt to teach, patient, in meekness instructing those that oppose them-*

> *selves; if God peradventure will give them repentance to the acknowledging of the truth; and that they may recover themselves out of the snare of the devil, who are taken captive by him at his will* (II Timothy 2:24-26 KJV).

There are three big things to note from this passage:

1. We can oppose ourselves.
2. We can be taken captive by the devil at his will.
3. We can be given repentance, see the truth, and recover ourselves from this captivity.

So many times we do things that we don't want to do. Likewise, we are not doing the things that we want to do. Some would say, "Go figure." I say, "Read II Timothy 2:24-26."

At times, it seems as if someone else is calling the shots in our life. He is. Satan was given a foothold and we were taken captive by him at his will. His entry was through a wounded place—the place of offense. It may have happened years ago. It should have healed by now, but our unwillingness to forgive has kept it alive and oozing like an active volcano. Pop psychology would call it a button. A big button that remains as sensitive today as when it was first introduced by a wound in our life. We feel like a marionette with Satan pulling the strings.

If this is you, here's the deal. You're not possessed of the devil, but you are influenced by him. Directly by him. It's like this. If I know that you have a wound on your arm, I don't have to touch it to get you to move.

I just have to make you think I'm going for it. That's a button. And the control of behavior lies outside of you.

BUTTON-LESS

Jesus didn't have any of these. Really. No buttons. Can you believe it? What an amazing guy. Amazing because He forgave . . . everybody. The equation below illustrates the connection in modern lingo:

Forgiving = No buttons
Choosing not to forgive = Buttons

The choice really is yours, but you don't have to do it in your own power. You can turn the page and learn from the Best. This time the invitation is His.

SELAH: CHAPTER SEVEN

What are some situations in which you acted like an oyster—covering up the irritation in order to deal with the pain?

Have you allowed twenty-four hours to pass before forgiving someone?

What poor choices have you made in order to cope with the pain of life?

CHAPTER EIGHT

JUST LIKE JESUS

How will we act if we're just like Jesus? What does that look like? What was it that Jesus did more completely and proficiently than any other human being—before or since?

I contend that the most Jesus-like characteristic was not love alone. God is love—clear and simple. The Bible says so (I John 4:8, 16). Yet it is not the love, but the manifestation of this love, that strikes me as so unique.

Is it holiness? We know that Mary's firstborn was the Holy One. The Book of Isaiah first displayed God as holy, holy, holy (Isaiah 6:3). This triple emphasis reinforced the magnitude and importance of this God-like quality. But it isn't His holiness that is so singularly profound to me either. Selfless love and pure holiness are expected of a God that exists as Spirit.

I am captivated by the Man who existed as flesh.

What was it about Jesus, fully God and fully man, that set Him head and shoulders above the rest of us? It's not speaking in tongues. Jesus never did that. It's not even performing miracles. He certainly performed miracles but so did the magicians of Egypt. Power over the devil? The disciples had this before they even received the Holy Spirit on the Day of Pentecost.

It wasn't power over the devil. It was the manifestation of a power over self. Jesus was a forgiver. He forgave. Everybody. Every time. They didn't have to ask. He didn't have to feel like it. No tears had to be shed. No hugs had to follow. He forgave because He knew, better than any of us, it was all about Him. It was *really* all about Him. If He had given place to resentment, even one time, the whole redemption plan would have been a wash. If He would have had one spot, we would have been without hope. It was all about Him because He was all about us.

I contend that forgiveness was the most Jesus-like characteristic. He sets the high-water mark. He holds the title. Many have done it, but none have ever done it better.

It wasn't easy for Him. He made sure of that. No free rides here. Jesus chose His lot in life. He chose how He would enter and how He would exit. Neither was too pretty. It was His to decide before the foundations of earth were ever laid. He set the stage and made sure that the ground was level. No silver spoons for Him and no excuses for us.

The brief synopsis of the Christmas story is that Jesus was the illegitimate son of a teenage girl in a small town. People talk now. People talked then. Although our world carries far less disdain over such a pedigree, the world of first-century Galilee was not quite as understanding. Illegitimacy separated you from high social standing, the family business, and your father's name.

You were excluded from social and religious activities. You were picked last for kickball. You didn't have to walk around and yell, "Unclean." Everyone already knew.

It was under these circumstances that He came. It was through these circumstances that He forgave.

The wonder of it all is that He did it! He faced everything we face—all of the rejection, misery, betrayal, and temptation—and still forgave. I heard a quote attributed to the late Ray Charles—"I didn't just play the blues. I lived them." Well said and the same could be spoken of the Lord. Jesus Christ didn't just teach forgiveness. He lived it.

I was recently in an editorial meeting when the subject of Christology came up. One of the men mentioned a perspective on Jesus that is worth noting here. He said that he believes Jesus' greatest temptation was to not use His immense power as God. He submitted Himself and refused to exercise His ability to alter situations and manipulate the minds of men. He chose to sleep on the ground. He chose to stay on the cross. He chose to forgive. He came here to live like us—and He did.

I mentioned this at the end of chapter three, but it bears repeating here. Jesus told his disciples that "the prince of this world cometh, and hath nothing in me" (John 14:30 KJV). The NIV reads that "the prince of this world . . . has no hold on me."

How empowering is that? It can be done.

The importance of forgiving cannot be overstated. Jesus reinforced its essentiality by making it one of the final actions of His life. The crucified Christ made seven statements. They were neither flippant nor easy to speak.

His back was flayed open and his ankles were nailed through to the cross. His battered body hung from the wrists and He was forced to use the spike in his ankles as the point from which He pushed His body up to gather breath. With each breath, His opened back scraped against the roughhewn wood. He had to work for every breath. Every word was labored. Mel Gibson's portrayal of *The Passion of the Christ* gave society an opportunity to reconnect with the savage nature of the cross and the magnitude of its agony. There was nothing easy about it. Every breath was an effort against unbearable pain. Under these excruciating circumstances, every word spoken was a word that mattered. "Father, forgive them, for they do not know what they are doing" (Luke 23:34 NIV) was one of the seven final statements. It had to be said. Not for them, but for Him. There was no spot of resentment before Calvary and there could be no spot of resentment after Calvary. When Jesus died, Satan still had nothing in Him. He was clean because He had forgiven. And because He died clean, we can live clean and whole and free. What a hope. What a model of forgiveness—a forgiveness that you and I can give to others.

The act of forgiving can become a daily reality in your life. You can be free from the manipulation of Satan. Again, I hear the naysayers, "But you'd have to be Jesus!" And my reply is, "No, you just have to have Jesus!" When Paul said he could "do all things through Christ who strengthens me" (Philippians 4:13 NKJV) maybe he wasn't focusing on healings and miracles. Maybe the primary "thing" was receiving the power to be just like Jesus and forgive.

SELAH: CHAPTER EIGHT

When you think about Jesus, what characteristic most often comes to mind?

What does that tell you about your relationship with Him?

Can you relate to the stigma and illegitimacy that Jesus faced as a child and teen?

If so, does it cause you to feel shame or hope?

CHAPTER NINE

EMOTIONAL SUICIDE

God shows up in the weirdest places. This time it was in the lobby of a Hampton Inn in Columbus, Ohio. I had just been dropped off for the night and was heading to my room. The December cold had cut through my light jacket and I needed a coffee for a quick warm-up. I did my standard desert coffee of two sugars and two hazelnut creamers. The coffee bar was adjacent to the large lobby television. The report of a tragic accident caught my attention. It sounded as if someone well-known had perished. As I repositioned myself in front of the TV, more than my coffee was getting stirred.

A small private plane had crashed during takeoff. The television flashed pictures of the wreckage against a backdrop of Colorado snow. Former actress Susan St. James's face filled the screen. She was talking about the tragedy. Pictures of her family appeared and the story began to take shape for me.

Her husband, Dick Ebersol, and their two sons, Charlie and Teddy, had just dropped her off in Montrose,

Colorado, and they were heading out to South Bend, Indiana. It was Thanksgiving weekend.

The runway was slushy and the air was mixed with light snow and fog. The Bombardier Challenger slid from the runway just before liftoff. The plane reportedly went through a fence and hit a roadway before the cockpit separated from the rest of the fuselage. Charlie, twenty-one years old, was thrown from the plane. His father and fourteen-year-old brother were still inside. Thankfully Charlie was conscious and bravely returned to the twisted wreckage. He entered the cabin through a hole in the side and found his father trapped beneath debris. Flames began to ignite throughout the plane as he pulled his father from certain death. In a moment Charlie returned to the wreckage to search for his brother and any other survivors. Teddy could not be found.

Charlie called his mother on her cell phone and she related the rest of the story.

Another crew member was pulled to safety, but Teddy's whereabouts remained a mystery. Within ten minutes the plane was engulfed in flames. The investigation determined that Teddy, trapped under the wreckage, was killed instantly and had not suffered.

It was now almost three weeks later. Ms. St. James related how she was sad, but not mad. In a very transparent moment, she related that her husband confessed his inner struggle, "It should be me. I've lived my life and Teddy didn't live his life."

People do that stuff. They blame themselves for living when tragedy takes someone whom they love.

Documentaries captured this during the post-9/11 saga. Men and women who were rescued from the World Trade Center were battling resentment—resentment toward themselves. This makes my brow furrow and my eyes squint. I lower my head and shake it slightly from side to side. How do we make that kind of connection? Why would we blame ourselves for living? Unspeakable grief? Searching for a sense of fairness? Maybe defying death rewires something in us. For that, I don't really have much of an answer. At least not one that fully works for me. I'm not sure how it gets on location, but I can recognize its arrival. Self-inflicted resentment. An unforgiving posture toward myself. This rational enigma certainly has proven to be an emotional reality.

Susan St. James followed up her husband's confession with a statement to her kids that made the floor of that hotel lobby become holy ground for me. God was saying something to me in that moment. He was talking to me through this lady and I knew it. She referred to the need to forgive yourself and stated, "Having resentment is like taking poison and hoping the other guy dies." She added, "Having resentments now—it's just gonna kill us."

WHO'S HURTING WHOM?

I observed the destructive nature of resentment during the fifth year of our marriage.

Melinda and I had recently moved to Newport, Rhode Island, to start a church. Redefining ourselves in a new city with new jobs and new ministry challenges prompted a marital spat or two. Not implying that we need those circumstances to have a barn burner, but this one made it to the record books.

Neither Melinda nor I remember the exact nature of the conflict or the words that were initially spoken. We do remember that something was said—and I said it. As I recall the moment, I think I could have hit Melinda in the face with a bat and not hurt her any more deeply. I saw the physical recoil of her face and the twisted expression of shock and pain. I hadn't merely crossed the line, I annihilated it. Whatever issue had been so pertinent instantly diminished in importance. I threw up the surrender flag. This argument was over.

I immediately apologized and tried to communicate my selfishness, shallowness, and feelings of betrayal to my wife. I had hurt her deeply. Maybe more than ever before. Immaturity overwhelmed me and I had said what I did not mean. I was truly sorry and begged her to forgive me.

MORE THAN SORRY

Early in our marriage Melinda and I agreed upon the protocol for granting forgiveness. The violator, usually me, would ask to be forgiven and the offended spouse would grant the forgiveness. Not so profound in principle, but this interaction was scripted in such a way as to ensure clarity and closure. It would go something like this:

Violator: "I am sorry for ____. Please forgive me
   for ____."
Violated: "I forgive you for ____."

The power of this is in the specifics. "I'm sorry"
alone does not get it. It needs to be said, but it is only
a precursor for the main event. We ask to be forgiven
for specific actions that cause specific hurts. On the
other side, "No problem—Forget about it—Don't
worry about it," won't get it either. These are too
vague. No closure there.

Given our example above I might say, "I am sorry
for being so insensitive and selfish. No disagree-
ment merits that kind of behavior. I am sorry for
not honoring you with my words. I am sorry that I
hurt you. Please forgive me for being so insensitive
and selfish, for not honoring you with my words,
and for hurting you." Typically Melinda would repeat
the points of the previous sentence and forgive me
for each one.

Not this time.

She looked at me and said, "That hurt too much.
I don't think I can forgive you now." (After all, she had
twenty-three hours and fifty-nine minutes to play
with!) All jokes aside, I had blistered her with my
words and she was having a seriously hard time doing
the very thing that she knew she should do. We had
agreed on it. She wanted to do it. But the wound was
deep and the words were not coming.

I excused myself to the living room and sat on the
couch. I began to flip through some magazines—
something that I never did. I had asked to be forgiven

and felt as if I were in the waiting room at the doctor's office passing the time until I was called in.

An amazing awareness came over me.

We had a modest apartment with a shotgun hallway. The five rooms and the entry extended from this long hall with three on each side. As I sat in the center room I heard it. It became louder and louder. More pronounced and definitive. It was Melinda. Actually, it was her footsteps. What it really was, was amazing. She was moving down the hallway between rooms. From the kitchen to the bedroom. From the bedroom to the bathroom and back to the kitchen again. She was stomping through the house and each step became progressively louder. Then she switched to punishing the pots and pans. Doors were slamming and pans were coming down on countertops. She was really boiling.

I felt fine.

The dichotomy of this arrested my attention. I was the one who had committed the offense. I was the one who should have been feeling all messed-up inside, but it was she. My wife's emotions were literally boiling— getting more unstable and bubbling higher and hotter with each passing moment. It was in that moment that Susan St. James' quote found life in our home.

Melinda's anger was not so much about what was said, but who said it. Her inability to forgive me indicated the depth of resentment that she was feeling. Having resentment is like drinking poison and hoping the other guy dies. I was definitely the other guy, but I wasn't the one in danger of dying. Melinda's resentment was actually manifesting in her actions.

Slamming pots and stomping across the floor. She was the pressure cooker. Not me.

Then it happened.

After twenty minutes or more, my sweet wife looked around the doorway into the living room and said, "I forgive you now." As God is my witness, the stomping stopped. Instantly. The pans were happy, the floor was happy, and I was happy. But we weren't the ones most in danger just prior to that moment—Melinda was. By pressing through to forgiveness she saved herself.

Resentment only hurts you. It was an afternoon that we would never forget.

SELAH: CHAPTER NINE

Who do you have resentment toward right now?

Let me restate the first question . . . whom have you refused to forgive within a twenty-four-hour period following their offenses toward you? (Write as many as you can think of.)

CHAPTER TEN

THE WHOLE NINE YARDS

Some scholars assert that "the whole nine yards" originated as a military term. The aircraft ammunition belts on a P38 Lightning were nine yards long and discharging the entire belt of ammunition was referred to as going the whole nine yards. The purpose of this chapter, and in fact the entire book, is to educate you and equip you to go the whole nine yards. They unloaded a clip. You and I will unload our hearts. From its original context this phrase is associated with destructive potential. Within the framework of forgiveness the phrase is charged with healing potential.

When dealing with offenses, we have to do it all— go for broke—don't leave a stone unturned. Or removed. Whatever slogan works for you is fine. The point is that we have to allow forgiveness to work for us and free us from the personal bondages of resentment, grudges, and bitterness.

The previous chapter outlined our personal forgiveness script. Specificity really does make a difference. It enhances communication, clarity, and consistency.

Some may feel as if a scripted apology is superficial. The apology may be superficial, but it won't be because it is scripted. The only repetitive parts are "I'm sorry for" and "Please forgive me for." You fill in the blanks and it will be the words you choose that will make it real or phony, deep or shallow.

And in case it's on your mind, who said you had to feel anything during this whole process anyway? I will address this more deeply during the chapter about the myths of forgiveness, but a quick mention right now could go a long way. Feelings of emotion can facilitate forgiveness. In some instances they might present a barrier to it. Since the act of forgiveness is a spiritual act, it goes beyond our physical and emotional states. I can be red with anger or pale with shock. My eyes can be flushed with tears or stoic with thought. My emotions are not the primary issue. I need the power of the Spirit to help me make the decision to forgive. The act is spiritual. It is a decision. People tend to throttle their forgiveness with their emotions and that is why so many continue to carry the anger of resentment and bitterness. Feelings are variables that affect me, but the act of forgiveness is beyond emotion. At least it can be.

There is a real difference between saying, "I'm sorry" and "Please forgive me." This book is really about the freedom we receive when we forgive someone, but this is a great time to discuss the part of the offender—the one asking for forgiveness.

When I was a middle school teacher, classroom management consumed the majority of my time. It seemed as if rudeness was part of the lunch menu and most of my sixth-graders were binging on it. One of my classes met just after lunch. The lunchroom staff dismissed students at different times and they straggled to class in waves. One afternoon two students arrived early. The boy was trying to flirt with the girl when she made a very rude comment about his height—or lack thereof. My students knew that rudeness was dealt with immediately and I demanded that they practice the forgiveness script that I used at home. I was finishing up my own lunch and a quick glance told her what I expected to be done next. She quickly said, "I'm sorry," and then went about organizing her book bag. Nice try.

"Good start," I said, "but you need to ask [him] to forgive you for the rude thing that you said about his height."

Her tentative reply was, "No way. I said I was sorry."

By this time several students were in the class. I had to get up from my desk before she said it and then the boy refused (for a moment) to forgive her. Just another day in fifth period! The point of application for us is that saying "forgive me" makes a difference. "I'm sorry" alone just isn't going to bring the same result.

This type of interaction brings closure. People are clear about what is being discussed. They are clear about what's on the table. They are clear about what remains as unfinished business. One person asks specifically and one person responds specifically. Feelings may not dissipate and wounds may still sting for a while. That's okay because those are emotional and physical things. The interaction of forgiving someone is spiritual. It starts in the spirit and begins the process of healing our emotional and physical pain.

Having discussed the *how* of forgiveness, now we need to talk about the *who*. (We won't be referencing the British rock band, unless, of course, they happened to have offended you in some way.) Maybe it would be clearer to say that we need to talk about the *to whom* of forgiveness.

To whom will I give it. When I started to type the last sentence my word processor superimposed a commonly used phrase for me to enter—"To whom it may concern." That's it. We need to identify the players if we hope to go the whole nine yards.

THE PLAYERS

The most commonly forgiven person is the perpetrator—the one who committed the offense. We easily understand his or her role in the situation. Without him, there would be no need to forgive anything. He or she is the abuser. The rejecter. The pastor. The parent. The friend. There is no specific moduf operandi for them. The common characteristic is that, in some way or another, these people hurt us. Maybe on purpose. Maybe with no knowledge whatsoever. Does it really matter? Knowing their motive may help us more effectively compartmentalize the situation in our minds, but it won't matter to our heart. We got hurt. Period.

It would be great if we could so quickly speak and act like Susan St. James. Living in the freedom of forgiveness—just days after tragedy took her youngest son. That really is wonderful. But we must remember that it is wonderful for her. In that situation, giving forgiveness is all about her. In your life, giving forgiveness is all about you. Remembering this and maintaining the perspective it brings will help us forgive those who have hurt us.

BLOWING OUR MINDS

This is wonderful in the truest sense of the word because it is full of wonder for us. We can't believe people do it. Have you ever seen an interview in which a victim's survivors offered unconditional forgiveness to the murderer? Have you ever caught yourself saying, "How do they do that?" Have you ever thought it? In one interview I heard years ago, the surviving parents answered our question—"[He] has already taken one life. We will not allow him to take another." The other life to which they referred was their own. They made a good choice.

So many people refuse to forgive because they feel as if it will dishonor their loved one or tie the hands of justice. Somebody needs to pay for my pain! That sounds good and it feels right, but it isn't. In fact, it's faulty reasoning from a faulty perspective. The facts are these: You have been hurt and someone deserves to be punished. You need to forgive and give up your right to punish. You will be setting a prisoner free. The prisoner will be you.

THE MAN (OR WOMAN) IN THE MIRROR

Speaking of you. . . . What if the offense you carry is directed at yourself? Oh sure, there was a perpetrator . . . an abuser . . . , but you blame yourself for allowing it to happen. Have you ever asked, "How could I have been so stupid?" or "How could I have let that happen again?" These kinds of questions put a bulls-eye on your head—one that you are aiming at.

So much of this is self-perception. People tell us that our line of thought makes no sense. Our rationale is ridiculous. It was not our fault. And still we wallow in our self-directed shame. If I would have been a better kid, my parents would not have divorced. If I would not have dressed that way, I would not have been raped. If I would have been worth loving, my father would not have taken his life. I should have called for help. I should have seen it coming. And on. And on. And on.

You need to let yourself go! When it comes to this level of forgiveness, there is a huge disconnect between the mind and the emotions. We often love the abuser so much that we choose to blame ourselves. The vicious cycle is that your esteem was already low—given your probable dysfunctional relationship with the perpetrator—and the abusive act only reinforced your feelings. They're feelings, friend. They're not facts. The reality is that you were a victim. Refusing to forgive yourself ensures that you remain a victim.

Forgive yourself. Say the words. Fill in the blanks of your own forgiveness story.

It's okay to forgive yourself for what you perceive. In fact, I encourage it. I just wrote that feelings are not fact. This is true, but it is also true that perception is reality. It sets the stage for the world you live in every day. It is your reality. Separating the two begins the healing.

You are not a bad person, but you treat yourself like you are. Forgive yourself for the things you perceive that you have done to hurt yourself. (That was a challenging sentence to *write* with clarity, and certainly a more challenging thing to *do* with clarity.) Challenging, but not impossible.

I met with a man several years ago who had been molested as a young child. The perpetrator was a relative and the act was so violent that the five-year-old boy's arm was broken. This adult man sat in the office and cried. He was consumed with shame. The irony is that he was ashamed of himself. I will never forget his words, "But I could have yelled. I should have done something."

I leaned forward in my chair and implored him to understand, "Man, you were five. You were five years old! You didn't have the physical strength, the mental ability, or the emotional stability to do anything. You didn't understand. It was your [relative]!"

He was with someone he loved and trusted. With someone whom he wanted to love him. He was five.

Some of us were twenty-five. In my experience, that only makes it worse. We are convinced that we should have known better. That's probably true, but mature gazelles fall prey to predators just like the young ones do. We have contributing circumstances just like the perpetrator probably does. Too often the abuser was the one once abused. Break the cycle! You can break the chain. Forgive yourself and let the Lord begin to heal the wound. He is the Master of restoration and you are a work of art that is well within His grasp.

THE OMNIPOTENT ONE

It is fairly straightforward to realize that we have to forgive perpetrators for their actions and ourselves for our perceived contributions. Accepting these two, although challenging at times, is not as hard to swallow as this third level. Especially for Christians.

I have some simple questions: Do you believe that God is omnipotent? Do you believe that God is all-powerful? Do you believe that God can do anything? Then why didn't He intervene in the situation that caused you so much pain?

If you've honestly wondered about that, then you might need to do some forgiving—heavenward.

Jesus knew that we could be offended at Him.

John the Baptist was sitting on the damp floor of a prison. His public ministry had been eclipsed by his cousin's arrival. John had been totally supportive of this shift in attention. His current situation, however, called for some reinforcement.

John sent his disciples to find the Truth.

They approached Jesus and asked the question of the ages: "Are You the Coming One, or do we look for another?" (Matthew 11:3 NKJV).

Jesus spoke for Himself. "Go and tell John the things which you hear and see: The blind see and the lame walk; the lepers are cleansed and the deaf hear; the dead are raised up and the poor have the gospel preached to them" (Matthew 11:4-5 NKJV).

Talk about letting your actions speak for themselves! What a supernatural, non-negotiable demonstration of power and incarnate authority. Sounds like a wrap to me.

Then Jesus continued with a postscript.

Oh, and by the way, fellas . . . "And blessed is he who is not offended because of Me" (Matthew 11:6 NKJV). The NIV captures His addendum this way: "Blessed is the man who does not fall away on account of me."

What is that little addition all about? The storyline was good, Man. No encore needed. No extra trailers. You've got the goods and You are the One. King of kings and Lord of lords. No problem with me. I'm sold. So why the need for that last line?

For years I could never understand why Jesus added that. Until I suffered.

You see, Jesus wasn't communicating to the crowd who was being fed. He wasn't even communicating to the faithful followers of John the Baptist. He was communicating to John. And John was in prison.

Essentially the message was this . . . I can do all things. I am fully omnipotent. I am the Messiah. I am the One. But Jesus was also omniscient and He knew that those messages would prompt more questions in His beloved cousin. So He responded to them in advance by acknowledging the likelihood of offense. Of offense "on account of [Him]."

We can't read about the return of those men. We can't read the story they related to John. We don't see them walk away from the prison and we don't see John turn and slump to the ground in despair. We don't hear his questions about fairness, justice, and salvation. We don't see him awake at night wondering why Jesus has time to save others and cannot seem to make time for him. The thoughts crush his mind and steal his sleep: "Did I do something wrong? Did I offend the Lord? What have I done to deserve such a senseless end? What glory comes to Him from this?"

I am taking a considerable amount of license with the story, but those questions weren't too hard to make up. I hear them all the time. I have asked them myself.

Jesus knew the questions were coming and acknowledged and encouraged in one phrase: "And blessed is he who is not offended because of Me."

Jesus acknowledged that He could offend us.

Jesus encouraged us that happiness would replace bitterness if we would choose to let it go. Remember, we are not resentful because of what was done as much as we are about who did it.

Jesus didn't do anything wrong to John. He hasn't done anything wrong to you, either. Allow you to be hurt? Sure. But it doesn't mean He did anything wrong. His ways are not our ways. He's God and we're not. Accepting this may not make you feel any better right now and it's not your ticket out of the prisons of life, but it will set you free from the prison of bitterness.

One of the most amazing parts of the story happened after the disciples returned to John. It was then that Jesus faced the crowd and spoke of John,

> *What did you go out into the desert to see? A reed swayed by the wind? If not, what did you go out to see? A man dressed in fine clothes?*

> *No, those who wear fine clothes are in kings'*
> *palaces. Then what did you go out to see? A*
> *prophet? Yes, I tell you, and more than a*
> *prophet. This is the one about whom it is writ-*
> *ten: "I will send my messenger ahead of you,*
> *who will prepare your way before you." I tell*
> *you the truth: Among those born of women*
> *there has not risen anyone greater than John*
> *the Baptist* (Matthew 11:7-11 NIV).

"More than a prophet . . . my messenger . . . there has not risen anyone greater than John."

Okay, Jesus. I believe in Your miraculous power and I can accept that You aren't going to save him from suffering. But couldn't You have said that last little bit while his disciples were close enough to take notes? Wouldn't that have been a nice gesture since he would never see You again in this life? That was a Hallmark card that never got sent. Jesus sent the message that John needed: "Blessed is the man who does not fall away on account of Me."

We have to accept the fact that Jesus will hurt us. He won't harm us, but we will suffer pain at His hand for the purpose of His kingdom. The Bible is replete with examples of this. My life is too.

The difference between hurt and harm is cited above . . . purpose. His purpose. Hurt is a by-product of growth and healing. We allow a surgeon to take a knife and cut us open. We submit to that knowing that we will have to endure weeks of painful recovery. Our movements will be limited. Our life will be put on hold. We accept the soreness and we accept the pain because it is pain with purpose. None of us want it, but a situation has arisen in our life that requires us to make a choice.

We choose pain because we associate it with a higher purpose for our health and future growth. It is pain with purpose.

Harm, on the other hand, is pain without purpose. That's the devil's territory. The wounds are senseless. Needless. There is no redeeming value. Jesus, because He is omnipotent and omniscient, brings redeeming value. He did it with Job. He did it with Joseph. He did it with Paul. He did it at the cross. He knows all about pain with purpose. Unfortunately, sometimes we forget that.

A HOME RUN

I taught these three aspects of forgiveness for several years before God revealed number four.

(I call this fourth aspect a home run because it helps us touch all the bases.) I was sitting at the soundboard during a prayer conference in Annapolis while a minister by the name of David Shatwell was speaking. I was in the balcony and I had my feet kicked up on the table and my chair was leaned back against the wall. Then he said it. My feet came down and my chair dropped to all fours. "You have to ask God to forgive them." I thought about that. It felt different from the other three. It was.

I realized that I was comfortable with forgiving the people who hurt me: others, myself, and God. I also realized that there was still a tinge of smugness, even self-righteousness, toward the human offenders. Simply put, I knew I could forgive them, but the justice of God would ensure they were punished. That felt good. I was acting righteously and justice would be done. Worked for me.

The problem was that Jesus had modeled more. The mentality that I had was not Christ-like. It wasn't the way Jesus would act. It wasn't the way He did act.

On a cross at Calvary He forgave His murderers. I had done that. On a cross at Calvary He asked the Father to forgive them. I had not done that.

I immediately began to think of people for whom I held resentment. The candle of the Lord was searching my heart and revealing the dusty corners. The floor was clean. The countertops sparkling. But the corners needed some work.

I believe in this stuff and I prayed it right then.

I have forgiven [them], Lord. Now I ask You to forgive me for my hidden, subtle resentments. For my self-righteousness. I pray that You would forgive [them] for the wrong that was done to me. I intercede on [their] behalf. I repent for [them] and ask you to cover [their] sin with Your blood. Do not hold this sin to [their] charge. In Jesus' name I ask it.

That's a whole new level, friend. It completes the cycle. It models our Messiah. It's the will of God for you to do.

SELAH: CHAPTER TEN

How are you with the idea of:

Forgiving the perpetrator?

Forgiving yourself?

Forgiving God?

Asking God to forgive the perpetrator?

Which of the four is the hardest for you? Why?

CHAPTER ELEVEN

MY STORY—PHASE TWO

They come in waves. "Cycles" might actually be more accurate. As the healing goes deeper and deeper, forgiveness will need to happen again and again. It depends upon the depth of the wounding, but, in my experience and in my observation of others, stones continue to surface. For Mother Earth it happens every year. At least in Connecticut.

I was conducting a community seminar in northeast Connecticut entitled, "Where Is God When It Hurts: Moving through Grief, Loss, and Disappointment." The concepts of stones applied throughout the sessions. During one of the breaks, a woman from the local church congregation approached me with a burning story.

I had been talking about the reoccurrence of stones in our lives and how it indicated a progression of healing at a deeper level. She concurred with the following account. A decade earlier she decided to start a garden. The ground looked good on the surface, but she quickly found that field stones needed to be removed. So she dug and tilled until a couple of feet of soil were stone-free. She had not unearthed enough stones to be very useful for fencing so she tossed them in a pile. As I recall, her neighbor was doing the same thing so they piled their stones together in the joint corner of their yards. Planting happened, things grew, and year one was a gardening success.

Then came year two. Excited about her previous success and knowing that she had done all of the tilling and hard groundwork during the first year, she went out to plant again. As she walked through the garden plot, something caught her attention. Stones. More stones. The pile in the corner of her yard was the same size so where did these new stones come from?

They surfaced from the ground. The ground that had been cleared out the year before. The ground that had produced a great garden just months earlier.

Well, it had been ten years when she spoke to me that afternoon. Her smile came from the fact that she and her neighbor had accumulated a pile of stones that would effectively hide a Volkswagen. (Her words—not mine.) That's quite a pile.

My points are these:

1. Stones continue to surface.
2. Growth will continue to happen as long as they are removed.

I learned this the "experiential way." I started to say the "hard way," but I don't know if there is an easy way. It all seems hard when you're in the moment.

It had been over five years since my vision experience at the altar. I had entered the ministry and had been successful as a youth pastor in Virginia and an assistant to the pastor in Ohio. Melinda and I moved from Ohio to Rhode Island to start a church. We were on-site, people were being filled with the Spirit, and lives were being changed. We enjoyed a vibrant children's ministry and the community was opening to our ministry efforts. I was a regional youth official. I was a pastor. I still had stones.

My altar experience years earlier was real. It was valid. It was right. My need for further healing in no way invalidated what had already happened. God was just taking me to a new level of healing.

Ironically, I had asked my pastor to visit our small congregation and teach about the principles of shame and emotional healing. I sensed in my spirit that our church was ready and that God wanted to introduce a depth of healing that they had not experienced. Too bad I was talking about myself!

The opening night of services arrived and I stood at the pulpit to welcome folks and give some introductory remarks. We met in a modest room at a Boys' and Girls' Club—folding chairs—portable sound system— a keyboard. Many folks knew about this particular round of services and several were still coming in at seven o'clock. I began,

> *I want to welcome you all here this evening. We are excited about having Pastor Wright with us and we are looking forward to his ministry. We will open with prayer in just a moment, Sister Smith will lead us in a worship chorus, and I'll turn it right over to Pastor Wright.*
> *Let's pray together. Dear Jesus . . .*

That was the last thing I said. Nothing else would come out. Emotion rose from within my chest and tears fell from my eyes. I leaned over the pulpit and began to cry. The crying turned to sobbing as I shook and gripped the edges of that wooden podium.

I wasn't really sure what was happening, but I knew something was going on. Something within my spirit was breaking. In retrospect, I realize that I had been wrestling with a feeling throughout the day that was just under the surface. Pastor Wright arrived early and we had spent the afternoon together. My humor was edgy. My wit was extra sharp. I must have been tossing one-liners right and left in a subconscious attempt to dodge what my spirit sensed was coming. Try as we might . . . those stones just seem to surface anyway.

Pastor Wright approached the pulpit and took my glasses off my face. He took my arm and walked me to the front row. I wasn't incapacitated, but I was pretty close. The funny part is that people were still arriving—walking in on their new pastor sobbing and praying in unintelligible sounds on the front row. That's what you get for coming late!

I had "thrown up" stones before, but this was going to start a series of healings that encompassed a four-year window. None of the others would be this physically dramatic, but seven more were coming. I don't really know what switch was flipped in my life to signify that I was ready for surgery, but it was. God had determined that I was ready to deal with the offenses. That's God's call. My job is to trust that He's smarter than I and that He wants me to be healed more than I do.

I had fluid coming from every opening of my face. I recognized God in it. I chose to trust until Pastor Wright spoke in my ear. "You have to go back to the grave and forgive your parents for dying." My head snapped around to the right and I looked at him through blurry eyes.

"What?" I questioned. He repeated it.

It struck me as being absolutely ridiculous. Do you think they died on purpose? They didn't leave me. They died! He was asking me to act as if they had discussed the situation: "I'll die in June and you die in July. The other boys are raised and out of the house with families of their own. We'll die three weeks apart and leave Andy. Sound like a plan?"

Again, with greater disdain, I asked, "What are you talking about?"

He offered an explanation, but three words sealed the deal: "You felt abandoned."

Talk about a spiritual act. My mind filed his request as ludicrous. My heart registered it as reality. The spiritual part of me had a choice to make. The Spirit of God was present to equip me, to empower me, to educate me. Class was certainly in session and it was test time.

In that moment I decided to walk by faith. I trusted my pastor. I trusted that he was with us in the will of God. I had felt that—I just thought it was for the others! I would take the first step. I would submit to the surgery of the Savior. I loved Him and I knew, in that moment, that He loved me.

I envisioned myself standing at the edge of that open grave. The sky was overcast. I was alone. As I choked out the words, "I forgive you for dying and for leaving me," something in me released. It felt as if thick leather bands were breaking from around my heart. I still cried, but it was softer now. I whispered it several times as I allowed forgiveness to work its healing. The beginning of this episode was almost violent in appearance. The wrap-up had a tender feeling to it.

I wiped my eyes and began to pray with others who had come with the hope of receiving the healing that had just happened to me.

DRAMA, DAD, AND A DIVINE INTERVENTION

A few months later I came across a story full of rodeo and ranching with a modern-day setting in Montana. The plot focused on the relationship of a dad and his son. The son was paralyzed in an accident while his dad was driving. The dad did not have a bio-logical father in the picture. A friend of the family, an uncle of sorts, filled the father role. There were angry words, tears, and a good bit of testosterone exempli-fied by the men as they struggled to save their family. The story climaxed during a county rodeo—a deter-mined dad appears at the last minute to team-ride with his son and win the coveted trophy while Mama claps and cries from the stands—hooray, hoorah! It was pretty cheesy. I think most people could have written the outcome after the introduction of the storyline.

I didn't think much about it until I started to cry. I was overcome with a shortness of breath, similar to a young child's quick breaths after he has cried very hard. Tears were squirting from my eyes and my chest was heaving up and down. I remained on the couch and looked at Melinda.

I asked her with choked-up words, "What is happening to me?"

She shrugged—her own cheeks now lined with tears.

After a moment of this, I wrapped my arms high around my chest, hugging myself, and lowered them to gain some sense of composure. The crying stopped.

I was so mad at myself. I knew better than to do that. I had gotten a hold of myself—literally. Something was coming up and I suppressed it. I literally suppressed the expression and regained control of myself.

At this point, I stood and wiped my eyes. I turned to Melinda and asked, "What was that all about?" I continued my monologue. "Maybe it was a dad thing. You know, I just wish I could have taken him sailing." Those words were no more out of my mouth when it all surfaced again.

This time I let it go.

The crying and shoulder shaking lasted a few minutes and passed like a summer rain.

You see, I was a sailor. We owned a twenty-one-foot sailboat. If you went out with me and you didn't know anything about sailing, your life was in my hands. It didn't matter if you were older, richer, or more handsome. You were counting on me to be competent and capable.

My dad never saw me sail. He never even saw me shave. He certainly never saw me as a man. Taking him on that sailboat would have meant that his life was in my care. He would have been looking to me, not as his little boy, but as a man. That revelation caused something to surface.

The doorbell rang. I walked down the entry steps of our apartment and opened the door. It was one of our church members.

"Got allergies?" he asked.

"No," I replied. "Just coughed up a stone."

Talk about an unorthodox messenger. God had just used a drama to bring a deeper healing to my life. I don't know why I'm surprised. He used a donkey. He uses me.

I could never remember the title so I figured I needed to find it so that I could give a specific reference for this chapter. I did my Google search and my jaw hit the floor when the title came across the computer screen. The title was *Everything That Rises*. Fairly appropriate considering it was the instrument God used to remove another year of stones.

These healing moments happened six more times over the next forty-eight months. Each time less demonstrative, but each time healing more deeply.

The last of the eight occurred in Peoria, Illinois, in November of 2001. I had been invited to join a team of pastors and was actually teaching this material for a regional conference. During the first break of the morning session, God decided that I would have my own break. Pastor Wright was the lead teacher and he approached me as I leaned against a side wall. He motioned for me to raise my hands and encouraged me to let the Lord go a little deeper. This time it was different. I didn't cry as much. I didn't shake at all. My hands were only halfway up, but my words were different. Different, in fact, than they had ever been before.

I said, "Mom and Dad, I forgive you."

Those around me didn't know why that was a big deal, but it was. "Mom" and "Dad" were what I called them. I had never forgiven them at that level of intimacy.

It was different than before. And so was I.

SELAH: CHAPTER ELEVEN

Have you ever noticed a feeling that you needed to forgive someone again for a previously forgiven action?

How did you do?

In what ways were the latter acts of forgiveness different from the previous ones?

CHAPTER TWELVE

THE SEVEN MYTHS

At least eighty percent of our pastoral care sessions require educating people on the subject of granting forgiveness. And it feels like eighty percent of those demand that we debunk the popular perceptions about forgiveness. I refer to these popular perceptions as myths. And they are popular. But just because everybody's doing it, doesn't make it right. Mom used to say, "If everybody was jumping off a cliff, would you join them?" In theory . . . no. In reality . . . most do.

These myths work because they feel right and that is the problem. Our forgiveness gets regulated by feelings. I understand many of the reasons, but understanding is not synonymous with acceptance. Some rewiring needs to be done. Our thinking needs to be recalibrated to better understand and actualize biblical, spiritual, and relational principles.

Wisdom can come from a process of failure or from a process of prayer. Let's go for the latter.

"Father, You are the Source of wisdom. All wisdom. I pray, in Jesus' name, that You would inject Your wisdom into my mind and my heart. Remove faulty thinking and replace it with divine understanding. Give me the mind of Christ so that I can forgive as You forgive. Amen."

THEY NEED TO ASK ME TO FORGIVE THEM

People withhold the forgiveness that they need to give because of pride. Here's the mantra: "I'm not taking the first step. They hurt me. I will forgive them when they ask me. They haven't asked me yet, so they must not want it yet." Those words drip with pride. The problem is that the need is not in them, it is in you. If you have been offended, then you need to forgive. Forgiveness is about you.

Did Jesus wait? Did He see more value in waiting for people to come to the foot of the cross to apologize or did He see more value in granting forgiveness to an angry mob and the vindictive priests who would never ask for it? Maybe the issue with this is time. Jesus knew He didn't have much left. We think we have years by the score. As usual, He was clear and we are clouded.

Offer unrestrained forgiveness. It is your gift to give.

I DON'T NEED TO FORGIVE GOD

"Why would I need to forgive God? He is a good God and would never do anything to hurt me."

Well, yes and no.

He is certainly a good God, but He will hurt you. And I don't mean He goes out for a coffee and lets

Satan hurt you while He's out of the office. I mean God authors the situation. It is by His hand and He is in control. He has a strong track record in this event that is worth noting. The event is personal growth and there is no one better at making it happen in our lives than God.

In a previous chapter I mentioned Joseph, Job, Mary, Paul, and Jesus Himself. Pages could be written marking the path of God's will in the lives of these people. I will just lift two from the pages of Scripture.

Job suffered a depth of loss that is irreconcilable. The money, the houses, and the camels were soulless commodities that could come and go. His children were not. Many Christians praise the Lord when the account of Job 42:15 is read. They rejoice at the blessing of having the three most beautiful daughters in the land. My tongue is usually silent.

I have a beautiful daughter and I pray for her every day—just like Job prayed every day for his kids. I don't know how she could be any cuter, but if God offered two daughters more beautiful than Emma, given the requirement that Emma would have to die, I would flatly refuse His generosity. How do you replace a loved one? Job received a double blessing of everything, but he still walked around gravestones that carried his name.

We rejoice at the account of Job 42:12:

> *So the LORD blessed the latter end of Job more than his beginning: for he had fourteen thousand sheep, and six thousand camels, and a thousand yoke of oxen, and a thousand she asses* (KJV).

Intellectual integrity requires that we give as much credence to the message of verse 11 as we do to verse 12:

> *Then came there unto him all his brethren, and all his sisters, and all they that had been of his acquaintance before, and did eat bread with him in his house: and they bemoaned him, and comforted him over **all the evil that the LORD had brought upon him*** (Job 42:12 KJV—bold type mine).

Job was a lot like us—he had some self-righteous issues. We'll be a lot like him—feeling some pain in the process of growth.

Jesus reinforced this theme within His inaugural sermon, "[The Father] makes His sun rise on the evil and on the good, and sends rain on the just and on the unjust" (Matthew 5:45 NKJV).

As humans, we define what is "good" or "bad" by the level of pain it brings. God doesn't.

When my pastor was in flight school, he had a boil on his knee. He tried to overlook the pain, but it simply became too great. The navy doctor cut the skin, lanced the boil, and drained the fluid. The process was painful. As the doctor was packing the wound, Lieutenant Wright commented that he was glad that was over.

"Over?" the doctor responded. "We're just getting started."

Two large corpsmen entered the room and stood at his side. The young lieutenant wondered why they were there. In a moment or two he found out.

The doctor began to press and push against the wound. Bro. Wright came off the table and was quickly returned to a horizontal position—thus the reason for the two men. The pain was excruciating. It lasted far longer than desired, but the core had to come out.

The doctor was doing what the doctor had to do in order to bring the healing that was needed. When the procedure was completed, Lieutenant Wright wiped the sweat from his face.

Almost thirty years later he related the story, "The pain of removing the boil was so intense that I would have chosen to live with the daily pain of keeping the boil."

That sounds fine for the short term, but it is really bad for the long haul. Keeping the boil could have introduced infection and required far more serious procedures, including the possible removal of his leg. Is that worth it? We often think so, but God certainly doesn't. Remember, He is the Great Physician and He will not require what we are not able to handle. He will never order a surgery if He knows there is the probability that we will not survive the process. If a human doctor would be so conscientious, can't you believe that our heavenly Father would far exceed that level of care?

God is all powerful and He is good. He deserves all the credit. All the credit. Maybe another way to put that is that He deserves credit for all things—the sun and the rain. There is an older Christian song that says, "If You're not Lord of ev'rything, then You're not Lord at all!" He is Lord of everything and it is this very quality which enables Him to bring eternal good out of temporal evil. When you begin to trust Him, you will begin to forgive Him.

I'M SUPPOSED TO FEEL LIKE IT

I don't keep scientific stats on this stuff, but I'd venture to say that we hear this myth five times more than any other. You don't have to feel it. Forgiveness is a decision empowered by the Spirit of God. It is not an emotional act, but a spiritual one. Quick question . . . do you think Jesus felt like speaking forgiveness while His blood soaked the rough timber of a cross? He was God, but He was man as well. It was a spiritual act. Feelings had to be unplugged in order for Him to maintain His inner wholeness.

It is so often the same for us. We want the feelings to go away so we can ultimately forgive. The converse is true. We have to forgive so that the feelings will ultimately go away.

ONE TIME IS GOOD ENOUGH

Satan's only real strength is deception. He can hinder our spiritual growth by getting us to do wrong things or by keeping us from doing the right ones. Forgiving is one of the right ones.

Some folks are of the opinion that they did it once, and they'll let us know when things change. Kind of like the husband who told his wife one time that he loved her. He said it on their wedding day and when things changed he'd let her know. Until then, what he said once is what stood. (An unfortunately true story.)

The reason this is faulty thinking with respect to giving forgiveness is because things have changed. We change. With every act of forgiveness we change. Multiple moments of forgiveness, even if the same words are said, are not exact actions. We are forgiving at a deeper level. I forgave my parents eight times during a four-year window. Each time was valid. Several times I said the same words, but none of them were repeats.

You'll know when God is calling you to a deeper level and asking you to forgive again. I look for a tinge of emotion. That's my "forgiveness thermometer." When I think about someone and there is a tinge of resentment or anger, I have come to recognize that it is time to forgive again. Even if that person is God.

I identify these moments of emotion by paying close attention to my physical responses. Sometimes my jaw tightens. Sometimes my eyes glint—which is cool if you're Clint Eastwood, but his characters probably needed to forgive a few folks, too. Occasionally the response is even more subtle—I feel a slight shift in my chest. My face is sober, but my heart is twisting. These are my red flags. They are just as telling for me as if I flew into a panic-driven rage.

They are my signs that I have more work to do. I have released the offense in the past—maybe even in the very recent past—but these signs are a call to a new level. There are stones in the garden and these blocks to growth need to be removed.

Melinda coined a phrase several years ago that has

really helped bring clarity to many. She says that for-giving is giving up our right to punish the offenders. We let them go. And when they hurt us again . . . we let them go. We take our hands from around their neck, we let go of the noose, we lay down the gavel. We have to forgive until this process is complete.

I was recently approached by a young minister who asked, "Don't you do forgiveness?"

"Well, I try to," I replied with a smile.

He introduced himself and told me his story.

He was asking for his mother. They had been aban-doned by his biological father and, as a teen, this young man had been wronged by the pastor's son. His mother had issues around forgiveness and he wanted to know if I could recommend any materials. I recommended a few resources, but since she wasn't in front of me and he was, I began to ask him about his own offense.

He mentioned that, years earlier, God arrested his attention in a dramatic way and took care of the offense. While he was praying at the altar, the visiting preacher grabbed a fistful of this young man's shirt and tie. He looked into his eyes and emphatically stated, "You have offense and if you don't repent, you are going to be lost!" Before this young man could respond, the preacher pointed to the side of that same altar where the pastor's son was standing and added, "And you're offended at him!"

Immediately the young man turned and fell at the feet of his peer and pastor's son. The tears poured from his eyes and the requests for forgiveness flowed from his heart. There wasn't an ounce of pride left in him. He wanted to be saved and was begging for forgiveness to make certain it could happen.

That was a definite God-moment. I rejoiced with him and then asked a question, "You were completely willing to ask for forgiveness *from* him, but how well have you forgiven him?"

For a brief moment, I got the deer-in-the-headlights look. A door had just been opened. This was a definite God-moment also and it was just as beautiful. This young minister's spirit was wide open and he demonstrated the same humility of which he had spoken just moments earlier. We began to talk about the specific dynamics of granting forgiveness and he began to grow right in front of me. Near the end of our conversation this fine young man asked, "How do you know when you've forgiven? I don't want to be around [the pastor's son]. Does that mean that I haven't forgiven him yet?"

I offered another of my forgiveness thermometers, "When you can enter a room where the person is and expend all of your energy making them feel comfortable and at ease . . . you're getting really close."

He looked up and revealed his honest heart, "I'm not there yet." Most of us aren't.

THE OFFENDER HAS TO BE LIVING

The main reason that people don't have to be living for you to grant forgiveness is because it is not about them. As long as you're breathing, the healing power of forgiveness can work. They don't have to be living. They don't have to ask. They don't have to be sitting in front of you. It would probably be nice if their ears were able to hear when you release yourself from the offense, but it is certainly not a prerequisite. The prisoner you set free is you.

THE PAIN WILL IMMEDIATELY GO AWAY

Remember the kindergarten chant: "Rain, rain, go away. Please come back some other day"? In this case, the precipitation is in the form of pain. Unfortunately, neither the rain nor the pain goes away immediately following forgiveness. Folks sure seem to expect it to.

Consider this: I walk up to you and pop you in the mouth. I begin to apologize profusely and explain that occasionally my arm just flies out in random trajectories. I ask you to forgive me. You understand that my action wasn't personal and you give me your forgiveness.

Here's the question that dispels this myth: When you forgive me does your face stop hurting?

I know the answer because I have the same type of face that you have! The sting does not go away. It will soften, but not immediately. Part of the problem comes from our unrealistic expectations. We maintain a bit of the idealism that if I do right, then God will do right . . . and remove my pain. Let me wrap this up by saying that God will do right, but He probably won't remove our pain. The apostle Paul prayed three times for his pain to be removed. Jesus will respond to our trial the way He responded to Paul, "My grace is sufficient for you, for My strength is made perfect in weakness" (II Corinthians 12:9 NKJV).

142

Take heart, friend . . . God is perfecting something in us and we are in pretty good company.

THE RELATIONSHIP WILL BE RESTORED

It would be so wonderful if all of our damaged relationships would be restored following our extension of forgiveness. The reason they don't is because we don't have control over the offender. They can thumb their nose at our act of grace or refuse to speak to us ever again. They may choose not to forgive and there isn't much we can do about it.

In cases like this, Melinda will ask you to get up from your seat and hug the lamp. Go ahead and do it now. Lay this book down and hug a lamp.

Did it hug you back? Why not?

Did you feel embarrassed? Why?

I know that the lamp did not hug you back and if you felt embarrassed, it was probably because someone saw you express an interactive action with an object that cannot interact. Lamps don't hug back. They can't. Sadly for some of us, we have relatives who just don't hug back either. For whatever reason, they can't.

Let me curb the frustrations of an unrealistic expectation by sharing this universal principle: You can only change yourself. No one else.

We only have control over our own actions and then we still need the Spirit of God to give us wisdom and direction to do what is best. If the once-broken relationship is restored, count yourself blessed. But try to remember their response is not in your power. Or God's.

SELAH: CHAPTER TWELVE

How do you feel about God getting the "core" out of your life? Write a prayer to God about your struggles with this.

Are you better at asking for forgiveness or giving forgiveness?

What will you begin to do to strengthen the weaker area?

CHAPTER THIRTEEN

THE ELEVENTH COMMANDMENT

I know. There are only ten . . . at least ten that are the biggies. We've seen the pictures with Moses and the stone tablets—five commandments on one side and five on the other.

There should have been eleven. It would have challenged the symmetry, but there should have been eleven.

These directives penned by the finger of God are not suggestions. They are commandments. Breaking them constitutes sin. Sin causes us to be lost. In my mind, anything that directly affects our salvation should be on the list. The granting of forgiveness certainly qualifies.

THE LORD'S (MODEL FOR OUR) PRAYER

Since I am expanding the Ten Commandments, it might be most prudent, on my part, to let the Author speak for Himself regarding the necessity of the eleventh:

> *After this manner therefore pray ye: Our Father which art in heaven, Hallowed be thy name. Thy*

kingdom come. Thy will be done in earth, as it is in heaven. Give us this day our daily bread. And forgive us our debts, as we forgive our debtors. And lead us not into temptation, but deliver us from evil: For thine is the kingdom, and the power, and the glory, for ever. Amen (Matthew 6:9-13 KJV).

That fifth request of the Lord's Prayer—"forgive us our debts, as we forgive our debtors"—is clearly emphasized. Still, the Master chose to make it His first point of commentary as He continued speaking:

For if ye forgive men their trespasses, your heavenly Father will also forgive you: but if ye forgive not men their trespasses, neither will your Father forgive your trespasses (Matthew 6:14-15 KJV).

That's Sermon on the Mount stuff. The concepts of Matthew 5-7 introduce the new message of the Nazarene. Forgiveness, therefore, is foundational to the message of the New Covenant and stands as a defining aspect of Jesus' salvation doctrine.

But there's more. We just don't always keep reading. Case in point. Jesus' words in Mark 11:24 have instilled faith in Christians for centuries. "Therefore I say unto you, What things soever ye desire, when ye pray, believe that ye receive them, and ye shall have them" (KJV).

Faith is awesome and necessary, but we need to keep reading into verses twenty-five and twenty-six if we hope to get a grip on the other "F" word—forgiveness.

> *And when ye stand praying, forgive, if ye have*
> *ought against any: that your Father also which*
> *is in heaven may forgive you your trespasses.*
> *But if ye do not forgive, neither will your Father*
> *which is in heaven forgive your trespasses*
> (Mark 11:25-26 KJV).

I'm all about the visual simplicity of equations, and this one is pretty straightforward:

$$\text{I forgive} = \text{I get forgiven}$$
$$\text{I don't forgive} = \text{I don't get forgiven}$$

Peter thought he had a handle on it and approached Jesus with the following, somewhat rhetorical, question, "Lord, how often shall my brother sin against me, and I forgive him? Up to seven times?"

Jesus said to him, "I do not say to you, up to seven times, but up to seventy times seven" (Matthew 18:21-22 NKJV).

Jesus exercised the liberty which He, as God, enjoys and attempted to further expand our concept with the following story:

> *Therefore, the kingdom of heaven is like a king*
> *who wanted to settle accounts with his servants.*
> *As he began the settlement, a man who owed*
> *him ten thousand talents [conservatively, ten*
> *million dollars] was brought to him. Since he*
> *was not able to pay, the master ordered that he*
> *and his wife and his children and all that he had*

be sold to repay the debt. The servant fell on his knees before him. "Be patient with me," he begged, "and I will pay back everything." The servant's master took pity on him, canceled the debt and let him go. But when that servant went out, he found one of his fellow servants who owed him a hundred denarii [just over three months' wages]. He grabbed him and began to choke him. "Pay back what you owe me!" he demanded. His fellow servant fell to his knees and begged him, "Be patient with me, and I will pay you back." But he refused. Instead, he went off and had the man thrown into prison until he could pay the debt. When the other servants saw what had happened, they were greatly distressed and went and told their master everything that had happened. Then the master called the servant in. "You wicked servant," he said, "I canceled all that debt of yours because you begged me to. Shouldn't you have had mercy on your fellow servant just as I had on you?" In anger his master turned him over to the jailers to be tortured, until he should pay back all he owed (Matthew 18:23-34 NIV).

Jesus concluded, "This is how my heavenly Father will treat each of you unless you forgive your brother from your heart" (Matthew 18:35 NIV).

The application of this parable far exceeds some equation of "don't forgive equals not forgiven." His message is much broader than that. Jesus introduced the concept of retroactive accountability. If I don't forgive, not only will I not be forgiven of current and future sins, but I will be held accountable for past sins that were once forgiven. No created being, human or supernatural, can take sins from under the blood. But, according to Matthew 18, God can. And will.

Heaping on all of the once-forgiven sins of my past wouldn't make me any more damnable. It's not like five thousand sins get you to the lake of fire any faster than five. Going to hell is not the point of the story. The top-shelf importance of forgiveness is! If I let the devil deceive me and I choose not to forgive others, I may be deceiving myself—thinking that the sins of my past are under the blood, when they're not.

What can wash away my sin?
Nothing but the blood of Jesus.
What can bring my sin back from under the blood?
Nothing but my choice not to forgive.

This is pretty heavy. For a lighter moment during ministry sessions, I often kid around by saying, "As a Christian, you have to forgive me. If you don't, you go to hell." Forgiveness, in this context, seems like it has to do with heaven, but it really has to do with now. It has to do with you.

Granting forgiveness is not optional.
Granting forgiveness is non-negotiable.
Granting forgiveness cannot simply remain under consideration.
Granting forgiveness is commanded.
I like to think of it as the eleventh commandment.

SELAH: CHAPTER THIRTEEN

Why is the granting of forgiveness the "eleventh commandment" for a Christian?

Are you being held accountable for previously forgiven sins as a result of your personal choice not to forgive someone?

Will you endeavor, by the help of the Holy Spirit, to forgive within a day?

AFTER WORDS

I believe that all the energies of a person's entire life can be for the concentrated purpose of a moment.

Every mile. Every tear.
Every smile. Every fear.
                    Every victory. Every trial.
                        Each experience,
            worthwhile.

They converge as part of a Master's plan,
            Extending like the fingers of a divine, steady
hand.

Melted together—revealing a rhyme,
            Pointing with purpose to a moment in time.

            A moment transcending our singular life—
            In a moment with clarity that cuts like a knife.

He causes our years of suffering to dim.
            Now pain with a purpose—our purpose in Him.

Ananias probably had a hardware store. He worked each week, went to church on Sunday, coached a Little League team, and read stories to his kids. My guess is as good as yours because none of us know anything about his life. Except for one afternoon in Damascus. He had an errand to run. A simple postal delivery . . . from Jesus Christ to the future apostle Paul. No big deal.

Why Ananias? What had life done to prepare him for such a moment of service? I don't know and you don't either, but we do know what he said to this blind gangster named Saul. In fact, we know the very first word he said to the murderer. Brother. He opened the conversation with the words, "Brother Saul."

I don't know what had happened to him, but he sure knew how to accept people and overlook their past. That kind of an understanding heart had been cultivated over a lifetime.

A lifetime of preparation for a moment of action.

That's how this book feels for me. It took twenty-one days to write and twenty-one years to live. The stories can now be labeled as pain with purpose. The purpose is to help you. I pray they have.

ABOUT THE AUTHOR

Andy Smith holds a master's degree in family studies from the University of Maryland with a bachelor's degree from the U.S. Naval Academy in Annapolis, Maryland. He is an ordained minister and serves as the administrator for Metro Evangelism in the Home Missions Division of the United Pentecostal Church International.

Andy and his wife, Melinda, have been serving "at-risk" adult and adolescent populations for over a decade and currently provide pastoral care services to congregations around the United States.

Andy's professional experiences range from administrating federal runaway services for metro youth, to counseling adult male felons, to teaching relational health concepts in both middle and high schools for Baltimore County public schools. Andy and Melinda have served on pastoral teams in Maryland, Ohio, Massachusetts, Rhode Island, and Virginia.

Their passion is to assist individuals and families in achieving relational health and spiritual wholeness through experiential and biblical principles.

They live in St. Louis, Missouri, with their toddler, Emma Grace, and black Lab, Sami.